Give Me Strength

by Nikki Talbot

Published by Mabel and Stanley Publishing
April 2024

 All the material and events are taken from the author's experience and are accurate to the best of her knowledge and recollection.

Join my FB group to stay in touch

About the author

Nikki is the award-winning founder of Pudding and Pie and has helped many schools and nurseries to teach children to be healthier and happier through food! When she's not covered in flour teaching children, she is a passionate motivational speaker dedicated to empowering women with a focus on motherhood, business and everything in between. Nikki helps women navigate through life's ups and downs.

You can contact Nikki on any of the ways below:

E-Mail nikki@puddingandpie.org.uk

https://www.facebook.com/groups/puddingandpie limited

IG http://www.instagram.com/puddingandpielimit ed

http://linkedin.com/in/nikki-talbot-80162822b

Dedication

This book is dedicated to Andrew my husband for always being by my side. For travelling this road with me. It's been one rocky road, filled with surprises around each corner and I am forever grateful to have you.

This book is dedicated to Charlie and Louie for making us both so very proud and being the greatest gifts that we could ever hope to have.

Last of all this book is dedicated to George. Our incredible dog that is always there for us with a cuddle and a lick to comfort us in the hardest of times.

With much love
Nikki x

"It is not the happy people who are grateful. It is the grateful people who are happy." **Anonymous**

Hello!

So why did I decide to write this book? I've always loved reading. I always got a little bit excited when I knew I could take out seven books at a time from our local library. I'd go trooping up the stairs, overloaded with my books and go to my favourite spot, leaning up against the radiator to escape into a new world. As a young girl of seven, never in a million years did I think I would be writing my own book!

From around my late 20's I felt I had a book inside of me. As life progressed and more and more 'stuff' happened to me I had an itch to share my story. So many things have happened to me, and I know that many other women and families have experienced difficult times, challenges and heartache; I want them to know that they're not alone. I want them to know that bad stuff happens to ordinary people, so much goes on behind closed doors that you'd never ever believe. Particularly as women, we can mask the real story. We are conditioned to wear many different hats, to juggle and multi-task multiple things at once. This book is for women who have experienced loss, for those that endure pain on a daily basis. This book is for you if you have experienced the 'giving birth prematurely rollercoaster', this book is for you if you are in business and have gone through the highs and lows that go with being an entrepreneur. Lastly, this book is for anyone that is the parent of a child with

a hidden disability. Regardless of what you may have been through, whether it's a similar journey to ours or completely different, I want you to feel supported.
This book is for you, for you to know that you are not alone. Whilst reading this, I want you to feel like a warm blanket has been placed over your shoulders to give you the comfort and support you so desperately need.

I have learnt many lessons throughout my life and experienced far more than most ever will. I don't say this as badge of honour - given the choice I would have always opted for "The Waltons" kinda life, but we don't get a say in how our life goes, or what path it takes. What we do have is a choice in how we respond to these experiences. I know without a shadow of a doubt that the challenges that have been thrown at me, make me the person I am today. Along with feeling supported and understood I want you to feel inspired. I am such an open book, that I have to be careful not to appear to be a victim, as this couldn't be further from the truth. Whatever happens to any of us you can bet your bottom dollar that there is someone far worse off than yourself. I consider myself incredibly lucky to have all that I do. When things don't go to plan, or you get thrown a few curved balls in life you really do appreciate every small thing. I have been extremely blessed to be supported by an amazing network of friends and family, far too many to mention individually but you know who you are!

Ultimately the reason I've written this book is for myself. If not one single person buys my book, I will still feel the relief of telling my story. At the time of writing this I am 46 years of age, and I cannot tell you how many memories and stories I have inside of me, waiting to be released.

Chapter 1

Life was very ordinary until I was around the age of seven. My family was made up of me and my two brothers, my mum and my dad, all living together in a semi-detached house in the midlands. This isn't a rags-to-riches story where I tell you how poor we were and about all of the things we had to struggle for. We would holiday in Torquay once a year, we had a dog, although in those days we certainly did not have takeaways or go out for dinner - but neither did any of our friends. My mum and dad had met very young, mum was 13 and dad was 22 and they were married three years later. They had us three kids very quickly and there was only 18 months between us. When I became a Mum myself, it was only then that I realised how hard it must have been for my mum. To have a three-year-old, 18-month-old and a newborn, sounds unthinkable to most!

The fact they got divorced was no surprise I guess when you look at how young they were when they met and how quickly they had us all. Their divorce was not amicable to say the least. There was a lot of angst, a lot of upset and I guess the easiest way to put it is that they didn't both want the divorce. Does an amicable divorce even exist? I guess it must be in rare cases where both parties agree wholeheartedly that they don't want to be together anymore, but this wasn't the case for my mum and dad. I won't go into the details as it's not fair and like any relationship they both have their own story. I remember crying myself to sleep and just praying like mad that they would get back together again. Sadly, we weren't the first family for this to happen and we definitely won't be the last.

Me, my mum and my two brothers went to live with our stepdad the same day that mum and dad separated and looking back, just got on with life as kids quite often do. There are two things that stick out for me during this time. The first is that I have a lot of regret for how dismissive I was of my dad. He only lived around the corner, but I rarely went to see him. Why I didn't, I really don't know. I adored my dad as he always made me feel so incredibly special. I was his only girl; I was his princess, and I can still to this day remember how small my hand felt in his. I remember times when us three kids would be playing up at night and my dad would come pounding up the stairs to "give us the slipper". (Yep, I'm afraid to say that back in our day, it was quite common to be hit with a slipper!) He would come into my room and pretend to hit me with it but instead slapped it onto the bed. Saying this out loud sounds ludicrous, bordering on abusive, but I thought it was funny! I'm not actually sure what he'd do afterwards when going into the boys room....I like to think the same but at the time

I was convinced that I had special treatment from daddy!

So, if I loved my dad so much, why didn't I go to visit? I remember the times when I did visit, my pile of Disney magazine subscriptions would be piled up to remind me how long it had been since I'd last visited. As an adult I look back and wonder if it was self-preservation. My dad was incredibly sad and bitter about the divorce. As a little girl I possibly didn't want to subject myself to this grief. He had gone from a family of five to now just him and our dog, Sandy. He told me afterwards how low he'd felt and that he had considered taking his own life many times.

Five years after the divorce, quite possibly one of the most significant moments happened in my life that would inexplicably form and shape the person I am today. This was my first experience of loss and even now over 30 years later I struggle to put pen to paper to describe the events.

Chapter 2

My dad decided to emigrate to Canada. He had family over there including his sister and her family. When I found out I was distraught. Canada was so very far away! He promised us he would send for us to go and visit him as soon as he'd got himself settled. Sadly, I didn't get to visit him until some four years later. I will never forget our last night together. We went for dinner at my now step mum's parents' house. I felt uncomfortable around them as I didn't know them very well and all I wanted to do was stay glued to my dad's side. Why hadn't I gone to visit him each week like my brothers had? If I'd have seen him more, would he have been happier, had more of a sense of family and not decided to go and live so far away? Back in these times (1989), flights were super expensive and so far out of reach. Only wealthy families were able to go off to Spain for their annual holiday back then, let alone Canada which seemed nearer to the moon than anywhere else!

Memories are strange things, aren't they? My version of a life event can be very different to yours, even if we were both in the same room at the same time. Memories can also be conflicting. An example of this is how I remember that when anyone asked me about my dad's life in Canada, I'd fill them in with stories of how he had learnt to ski and sail and how cool was that? I'd proudly tell them that even though he was a working-class mechanic (in those days you weren't that wealthy being a mechanic as not many people set up on their own) he now owned a beautiful home and had an incredible lifestyle. I do remember how proud I was, but I also remember how eagerly I'd wait for his letters to arrive. This was way before the internet had arrived. The letter was very distinctive as it was written on blue paper that folded on itself to make an envelope all in one. As soon as it arrived, I'd scurry upstairs to my room to devour it in private. My dad's big loopy handwriting told me stories of what felt like a faraway land and of all his adventures. I'd write back immediately filling him in if what I'd been up to. Desperately trying to make my life seem way more exciting than it was! Whenever he'd call, he'd always tease me with my 'brummy' accent, and I couldn't believe how Canadian he sounded so quickly.

Dad broke my heart when he left, and I guess there would never have been a good time to do something like this but looking back, it felt like a very hard time. I'd just started secondary school; I'd left all my friends behind as I went to a school that wasn't the feeder school at the time. Hormones and such monumental changes all happening at the same time were undoubtedly going to have an impact on me. Only later in life did I realise how much I'd put my dad on a pedestal. How I'd made him into my very own real-life superhero. He was my first significant male relationship, and this would play a pivotal part in my relationships later on in life.

From a young age I had a very close relationship with my mum. I also have a lot of respect for my stepdad. He took us three kids with all of our baggage and never moaned. I guess he must have loved my mum so very much.

Chapter 3

As things were so acrimonious between mum and dad, we ended up escaping to Bristol for a short time to stay with my stepdad's sister. I'll never forget the day I was called out during the middle of the school day to go home with my mum. I didn't realise that this was the last time I'd see my friends and wouldn't get a chance to say goodbye. Looking back this must have been hard for my little seven-year-old self as I remember writing letters to my friends telling them how much I missed them and could we still be best friends.

This sudden move to Bristol was pretty significant for me and my two brothers as we went to a school there for six weeks and absolutely hated it! It's hard enough to join a new school halfway through the year when everyone else knows each other, but it feels ten times harder when you don't have the same accent. Talk about sticking out like a sore thumb! Funny isn't it how as a kid all you want to do is blend in and be the same as everyone else, yet as a parent I advise my boys to follow their own path and not to be a sheep!

After our stint in Bristol, we settled into a school in Lichfield which I enjoyed. It was a lovely area and a fabulous school. Unfortunately, our time there was short-lived as we moved back to Sutton Coldfield some 12 months later. We finally settled down and

I absolutely adored my time at the local primary school and remembered how I thought my heart was going to break when I left. None of my friends were going to go to the same secondary school. I was one of eight children going to our new school and only one of those was a girl; and she couldn't have been more different to me.

I honestly think that changing schools and moving houses as much as I did really helped me be the person I am today. I adore meeting new people and finding out about them. I hate seeing anyone sitting on their own, so I have to go and chew their ears off and find out about them! That's not to say that I don't envy others' idyllic childhoods where they had the normality and security of not moving schools and gaining friends for life. I lived in 15 different houses as a child and teenager which may explain why as an adult, I've moved around far less and stayed in just two family homes over the past 20 years plus. I crave security in every sense. Everything I do now is to build security for me and my family.

So back to secondary school life. I did my usual and made some great friends, but it didn't come quite as easy now that I was a teenager and amongst new friends who had known each other since they were 4. I remember hiding in the toilets on Wednesdays and Fridays when my two and only friends were both at drama club and I had no-one to hang out with. Why I didn't just join the club I have no idea!

By this time, I had learnt to be pretty street wise and independent. My mum and stepdad had gone on to have two of their own children and I was the second eldest of five (My older brother Scott was only 18 months older and agrees that I was the bossy older sister!) Whilst me and my two brothers have a lot of shared history, I've always considered my younger brother and sister as my siblings and never called them a half-brother or half-sister.

I remember when my brother James was first born and how much I absolutely adored him. I was nine and so the perfect age to be a "mini mum" and care for him. I loved nothing more than taking him out and looking after him. I remember taking him on the bus into town to price up the school uniform for mum and got a few dirty looks from others as I probably looked like a very young mum. How opinionated can people be? Why's it their business? We are talking back in the late 80's now and I had always looked a lot older than my years. It was always me that was pushed into the shop to go and get the booze as I looked old enough and this was way before ID was asked for.

I was there for my younger sister Ellie's birth and always felt a strong bond with her. Whilst the gap between us was pretty big as I was 16 when she was born, we have since become super close as we've gotten older. I'm sad that I didn't get the same growing up and living together memories. Ellie was 3 when I moved out, but I'd like to think our bond since has made up for that.

My mum had brought me up very liberally. She had always let me have a half glass of wine at the table on special occasions which in that day and age was unheard of. Most of my friends were sneaking out with booze but I never needed to do that. Later on, in life my mum openly talked to me about sexual relations and went with me to the doctors for me to go on the pill. I guess because she had been a young mum herself, she understood how life could be and didn't ever want me sneaking around. I'll always remember her telling me to call her if I was in trouble and she would come and get me. She didn't want me to be afraid of calling because I was somewhere I shouldn't be.
I was older than my years and caused some controversy by going out with a boy two school years ahead of me. He had broken up suddenly with his long-term girlfriend to go out with me which didn't make me too popular with the Y11 girls at the time. It all worked out in the end though as we split up after a few months and he went back out with her!

Chapter 4

I met my first significant boyfriend when I was 16 and was smitten. We spent every available moment with each other. Thank goodness we met just before my GCSEs as I did fairly well with them but not so good with my A Levels.
We were together for three and a half years before we split up very suddenly. It was over something very silly and, whilst it was officially a joint decision, it was so very far from what I wanted. I spent the next few weeks and months pining for him, desperate to have him back. At the same time as this happened, my mum and stepdad were going through real difficult times. We had gone through a recession and my mum had had to sell her business to support my dad's, but it wasn't enough. They had to file for bankruptcy and our world was about to change significantly. We had been very fortunate to live in some beautiful homes, go on holiday multiple times a year and both my brother and sister were in private education. At this point I was at Uni and whilst I didn't have too much money, I did have two part time jobs. Like many families at around this time, we had big changes. We needed to sell our house to move into something much smaller, all of the luxury holidays had to go, and it was now beans on toast multiple times a week. Mum and dad were under a lot of strain. They had us three teens, as well as two younger children (we were 21, 19, 17, 10 and 2

years of age) Can you imagine the stress? Managing a blended family with a load of hormones, bankruptcy, and very young children? My mum also had gone through a lot with her health and undoubtedly had a lot of hormones to contend with herself.

I remember sitting down to have a family meeting and I offered to go and try and find halls or somewhere to live whilst I finished my studying. We moved to rent a small three-bedroom house. It was cosy to say the least as there were seven of us!

I guess looking back it was a perfect storm just waiting to happen. All of this going on at home whilst my relationship broke down. I was in a very dark place, anything that had previously been stable had come crashing down. I'd even moved universities as I realised that my course wasn't quite right so quite literally every aspect of my life from the home I lived in, to my first love ending had changed.

One night it became too much for me and I took an overdose.

There are usually one of two reasons someone takes an overdose (broadly speaking.) The first is a cry for help because you need to let others know how bad you are feeling and that you need help and the second is because it's too painful to carry on life as it is.

I remember sitting upstairs in my room and feeling so incredibly down. I could hear my family downstairs watching tv and laughing about something. I had never felt as lonely as I did at that moment. After swallowing a lot of pills, my brother came into my room and instantly knew something was wrong. He rushed down the stairs to tell mum. I'm so sorry Dean as that must have been a terrible shock for you and not something that anyone wants to go through. I have an incredibly strong bond with my brother, and I think serendipity played a part in him seeking me out. Did I do it as a cry for help or was it because I really didn't want to live anymore? I'm not sure.....all I do remember is waking every day with that cold dread of realisation of how my life was now, and I didn't want to feel that pain for any longer. I don't blame anyone for my actions other than myself and I am 100% responsible for myself.

It was a massive life lesson. I had put my boyfriend on a pedestal and that was never going to be a healthy relationship long term. At the time I was only really happy if I was with him and that is so incredibly unhealthy. As I alluded to earlier on, my dad emigrating at such a pivotal age undoubtedly was a factor. Never ever again have I relied on anyone else for my own happiness. The only person that is responsible for my happiness is me!

I am forever grateful to my brother finding me and for getting speedy help. I absolutely adore my life that I have now. It is for this reason that I get so upset when I hear of someone else taking their own life. Especially if that person is young and has all their life ahead of them.

Chapter 5

Shortly after this time, we moved to a teeny tiny new home. Well, it was probably just an average sized house, but it was tiny for all of us seven to squeeze into! My mum and dad had their own room, my sister and I shared a tiny room. My bed lay underneath my three-year-old sister's bunk bed, and I remember I was fine if I laid flat, but every time I tried to turn over in my sleep, I'd bash my legs! Worst of all, my three brothers shared a room. They were 20, 17 and 10 so you can only imagine how cramped and difficult that was. I had changed my degree course, so I was now at a different Uni and didn't really know anyone; I was starting again. After my split from my boyfriend, I became friendly with a great bunch of friends that I am proud to say are my super close friends almost 30 years later. I guess looking back, I went off the rails a little. I discovered the "all-dayers" with these girls, started smoking and was enjoying all the benefits that escapism brings. I was escaping my heartbreak and diving into a new world. Things were going to take a turn for the worse just around the corner. Very sadly, one of my close friends lost her boyfriend very suddenly and his funeral was on my birthday. As 19-year-olds do, we got very drunk that day and I managed to lose my key. I came stumbling in, waking my mum and dad up and it was the straw that broke the camel's back. They asked me to leave the house as they couldn't take it anymore. I remember feeling very let down and lost. I tried to call my dad in Canada to ask for some help, but he didn't feel he could do anything to help whilst I lived so far away. Within days I moved to a shared house in a run-down area. I could just about manage to scrape through my bills as I was working two part-time jobs whilst still studying.

I remember one isolated incident sitting at a bus stop after attending a lecture and feeling so incredibly lonely. My life as I'd known it had crumbled and I really didn't recognise how my life had turned out. Within just a short few months, I had split up with my first love and gone from a pretty comfortable life, to now living in a small bedsit on my own, in an area I didn't feel massively safe in. I don't remember feeling sorry for myself at the time, other than this one moment, but I do look back to that 19-year-old and feel sorry for her. I feel that she had a burden to carry and I'm so very proud of her.

At the time I was very upset with my mum and dad as I felt that they had let me down when I needed them most. It's only now that I'm a mum that I can appreciate some of the pressures they were under. My mum had five children, three of them were teenagers whilst the other two were very young. Each stage of being a parent is hard, whether it be caring for young children with their energy and tantrums or terrible unruly teens… it's hard. To have both going on at the same time is unthinkable. Add to this the fact that we were a blended family so there was plenty of "you're not my dad" flying around and then a huge grenade of financial difficulties. No wonder things went as they did. I'm not responsible for my mum and dad's decisions, but I am for my own responses. I had turned rebellious and had always acted like I was five years older than my years. I always wanted to be at that next stage, drinking and going out way before most of my peers; having an older boyfriend whilst most of the girls in my year were happy going on dates with one of the lads in their class at school. I guess I was pushing any boundaries that there were, and it wasn't easy having me and my brothers coming in at all hours whilst having younger children at home. I was extremely vulnerable after attempting to take my own life and being ejected from the family home was a stark realisation, I was responsible for me, no-one else.

Over the course of the next three years, I finished Uni, and worked in a series of office jobs from banking to recruitment. I moved out of the horrible bedsit to nicer shared houses and even managed to live with one of my best friends in a flat together for 12 months. This was a massive learning curve for me. I was learning to budget and fend for myself and dip my toe into the world of work. We had plenty of laughs as I worked with a couple of best friends in the same bank.....not that we got much work done! Our whole focus was on when we were going out next and could we get through the day with a raging hangover. Looking back at this time in my life it really taught me how to look after myself. I had to grow up fast, learning to manage my money and be on time for work. I met my, "to be" husband some three years later and I can honestly say that it was the right time. I'd had a few years to learn to be on my own, to let my hair down with the girls and if we'd met any earlier, I wouldn't have been ready to settle down.

Chapter 6

It was now 1999 and I met Andy at work, as so often people do. He was great for me as he was a strong character and certainly wasn't a yes man. When my dad came over from Canada to meet him, he remarked upon the fact that Andy was my alpha male to my alpha female. Over the years I've thought back to this a lot as Dad was right. What this means is that there's never a dull moment and it can be quite fiery at times! When we married in 2004 not for one moment did I realise how much we'd go through together. Andy has always remained by my side, through thick and thin, for better or worse, and for that I am so very grateful. Currently as I'm writing, Andy has been diagnosed with Cancer and I couldn't be prouder of him. He's so incredibly strong and has totally carried on, battling his way through the intensity of chemotherapy. Anyone that has gone through chemo will know how gruelling it is. He has continued to work and get on with life as normally as possible and I'm so incredibly proud of him.

We always knew we'd want a family of our own and like many women, I just assumed it would happen quite easily. Looking back, I guess there were signs that things were not going to be straightforward for us, but I was pretty naive. After I had split up with my boyfriend and gone through the difficulties of leaving home my periods stopped altogether. I remember going to get checked out and was told that this can happen when you've had a big shock or something major happens in your life. Weirdly enough they didn't diagnose me with PCOS until some years later when we were trying to conceive. My periods did return so I wrongly guessed it would work out. Like most things in life when I set my mind to do something I will research the hell out of it to make sure I achieve what I've set out to do. I learnt how to track my dates so that I'd know when the optimum time would be to conceive. I bought the urine stick so that I could figure out which days I'd be "good to go"; I showed my one friend how to do the same and it worked for her straight away so I just couldn't figure out why it wasn't happening for me. I had a brilliant boss at the time who advised me to go and visit a Dr privately to explain the situation and it was there that they diagnosed me with PCOS (polycystic ovaries syndrome) and this was the reason that I was not ovulating. If it wasn't for this person encouraging me to go and get checked out, I'd never have known that I wasn't ovulating and would be unable to conceive naturally so thanks so much Vicki!

I remember going to Italy on our first wedding anniversary and being in tears as I just didn't understand why it wasn't working. To compound this on our return our close friends were now also pregnant after coming back from their honeymoon.

It happened to them instantly. We had got together to meet up, to hear all about their honeymoon, and they were a little apprehensive about telling us their news as they knew how hard we had been trying to conceive. This was now two of my closest friends pregnant together and I really felt for them as they were worried about telling me! I'd be lying if I said it didn't hurt as I just couldn't figure out why it wasn't happening for us. When we found out we were expecting identical boys we were shocked to say the least. There were no known twins in the family. I had a scan as soon as we'd found out that I was pregnant which was pretty upsetting as they couldn't find a heartbeat. I remember going straight to my friend's house and crying my eyes out. What the sonographer had failed to tell me was that at five weeks pregnant they wouldn't expect to see a heartbeat! I went in to have another scan because I had intermittent bleeding. When I was around 10 weeks pregnant, we went to have a private scan and it was here that the sonographer assumed we knew we were expecting twins! I'll never forget how casually she told us…. "And here's baby number two's heartbeat." We were like, "Whaaaaaaat?"

Our disbelief and shock were further extended when we were ushered into a room with a serious consultant who told us that our pregnancy was a risky one. The fact that identical twins share the same placenta, means that there is a high risk of twin-to-twin transfusion. This is where one baby can over-consume whilst the other twin becomes malnourished. This meant we would need regular check-ups to keep an eye on things.

Once we told our families and friends, the shock began to subside, and we were very happy as we began to make plans for two new arrivals into our life!
Regular scans were made, and all seemed fine until I reached 25 weeks when I was rushed into hospital with bleeding.

It became very apparent that I was indeed in labour, and our boys were ready to arrive!

Chapter 7

If going into premature labour has happened to you, you will understand how surreal it all is. Doctors & nurses rushing around, all very concerned and heated incubators at the ready!
I'll never forget the sight of the two incubators at the foot of the bed with two pairs of knitted hats. Two pink and two blue as we didn't know whether we were having boys or girls. All we did know is that they were going to be two of the same.

I had a friend who was a midwife working at the hospital and I asked if she could come and see me if she was on shift. I needed to find out what the babies' chances of survival were. For some this may sound unbelievable, but for me I needed to prepare myself for the worst.
Liz held my hand, looked me straight in the eye, and very kindly told me that the chances of both surviving were not great.
I needed to hear this.

Weirdly enough it spurred me on to do my absolute best for them.
I still cannot explain the feeling of being in labour and trying to keep our babies in. It was so unnatural and goes against everything your body wants to do. Most women go through the pains of labour with the end goal of getting their babies out. For us it was the opposite, we needed to slow

everything down to allow time for the meds to help their lungs strengthen. This meant (at the time back in 2006) that we needed 24 hours in between two doses. It was imperative that we did this as it would make a massive difference on their chances of survival in the outside world.

After over two days of being in labour, the decision was made to bring our boys into the world. It looked like twin two was in distress and there was a possible infection. It felt so wrong to be forcing them out when they should have been growing inside me for another 15 weeks.

Charlie & Tom were delivered naturally (if you can call it natural in theatre with 14 doctors and nurses milling around) on 28th April 2006. They weighed 1 lb 14 and 1 lb 12 respectively just 12 minutes apart.

I remember this time so vividly as if it was only yesterday. Andy was super excited, and I was highly irritable and so very down. This was not what I envisaged our birth to be. The “Pampers baby” that I had imagined was a far cry from our reality. Our babies didn’t look like babies. They looked more like two tiny animals with a light covering of downy fur that they have to keep them warm. Now they were here, all I could feel was despair. How could these tiny things covered in masks and wires survive? I remember my second night after being transferred to the Q.E to follow the boys as if it happened yesterday. We had a private room and Andy was allowed to stay with me. I remember lying wide awake in bed and feeling so very lonely. If Andy had said to me at this point, "let's escape," I would have gladly taken his hand and ran. As I am typing these words, I am deeply ashamed of myself. My hormones were raging, my milk was coming in, so my boobs were engorged and killing me, and I was in a lot of pain as I had been cut open to allow the safest delivery for our boys. Looking back, I guess I had been living on adrenaline and had been very focussed on getting the boys into the world as safely as possible. Give me a challenge and I'll do it. Now we had achieved this I was lost……I was not in control of what happened next.

Chapter 8

Our life in SCBU (special care baby unit) was the rollercoaster you'd expect with far more lows than highs. Our boys were transferred to Birmingham Women's Hospital (BWH) where they were equipped to look after "extreme prems," as we'd learnt our babies were now referred to. The first time I walked into the SCBU I had an extremely sobering discussion with the Head nurse. She told us in no uncertain terms that they were not there to keep babies alive just for the sake of it. They wanted to ensure that every baby that survived would have a good quality of life and that it was not a given that this would happen for every baby that came into the unit.

Every day we would walk into SCBU to learn of a new development; this may have been the fact that one of their lungs had been damaged by the ventilators, there was a worrying shadow over a brain scan, or an infection. Even a common cold could kill them, so we had to be extremely careful. We were advised not to allow hope that they would both survive. I tried so very hard in those early days to steel my heart and not to fall in love with them. There was a pivotal point for me at about three days, whereby I decided I couldn't carry on in this way and no matter how long we had with them I would give them both my undivided love and attention. Even though the boys were not at home with us, I was very busy! I had been advised to express my milk every two-three hours as that would be what I'd be doing if we had the boys at home and my body needed to get into this pattern. If you have ever breastfed, you will know that the more you feed (or in my case express) the more milk you will produce. I knew that this was the one thing that I could do for my boys, and I was going to make sure I diligently stuck to the routine. I ended up expressing so much milk that I was able to provide milk for other mums in the unit who were not able to do the same for their babies. This may sound a bit weird, but all of the milk is sanitised. There were times that I felt this was hard as I would set my alarm every 3 hours to express, and the machine looks like something you may use to milk a cow! Having a warm and snuggly baby to cuddle up to in the middle of the night was not my reality. I used the time wisely though and like many serial multi-taskers, I entered a new world of forums and read about other peoples' stories of their special care baby journey. These stories and blogs helped give me faith that I wasn't alone and there was a chance that it would all work out.

We were shown how to change their nappies and the sight of Andy doing this so unbelievably tenderly is one that I will take to my grave. When you have babies that are born so early, they live in closed incubators with two holes either side. When administering meds, adjusting tubes or bathing them, you put your hands into these holes to tend to them. It's quite tricky and not least of all because they are so teeny tiny. How I try to describe the size of them is that their full face from hairline to chin was the same size as the length of the tip of my thumb to the second joint. Have a look at your thumb now and you will get an idea. If they were fully lying flat, they would be about the length of a Sky remote control. As you can imagine, their nappies were specially commissioned by Pampers and were minute.....You could fit a nappy in the palm of your hand.

After around six weeks, the hospital felt that both boys were doing well enough to be transferred to our local hospital. This felt like a huge blow to us. We had spent 24/7 with the doctors and nurses caring for our boys and we did not want to move, let alone the disruption an ambulance journey may have been for our boys.
Eventually we caved in, with the belief that the boys would be cared for by doctors that would get to know them and care for them once they were out-patients. Whilst no-one actually said the words, we were definitely given a "nod and a wink," that this was a positive move and a step towards bringing them both home.

Sadly, this was not to be the case as just 10 days after them being transferred to our local hospital, Tom died very suddenly.

Chapter 9

I will never forget the day that Tom died. It remains a crystal clear, sharp memory to me. For those that have ever lost a child you may feel the same. A big part of me doesn't want to forget any detail as his memory is all that we have left of his short life.

When the boys arrived, we had been showered with cards and gifts that I had tucked away into another room out of sight. I couldn't bear to open anything that may look like I was sending a sign to the universe that I was taking it for granted that they were here to stay. They had stayed in this room untouched for almost two months. I had not bought one single nappy as I hadn't dared to hope or believe that our babies were ours to keep and bring home.

I guess by the fact that we had been given the nod and wink by the BWH, and that they had been transferred to our local hospital, this gave me some courage to do what I did on this fateful day. I decided I was going to go and start buying some of the clothes, nappies, and equipment that these two babies would need. This was a massive deal! I was also going to be leaving them for the longest time I had at this point as I had pretty much been by their side, just going home to sleep. I went in super early to breastfeed Tom as ironically it was Charlie that was not feeling too well. He had an infection and I had been advised to leave him to sleep in his little incubator. I remember the doctors doing their morning rounds and remarking on the fact that they didn't need to check him out as he looked so healthy and content. I was having a little cuddle with him, whilst I breast fed. I've asked myself a hundred times since, would they have picked up on something if they had checked him out? I guess by the fact he was breastfeeding, they felt it was a sign that all was well. How wrong they were. I then went off to the shops and bought "all the things". I remember feeling a mix of nerves and excitement as our dream started to feel a little more real. We even got the double pushchair out to assemble and understand how it worked! This was a monumental day……little did I realise quite how monumental and completely for the wrong reasons. I came home to express my milk and put a call into SCBU to see how they both were doing. I remember speaking to the sister on duty at the time and she told me how well Tom was doing. They had left him off his CPAP for six hours at this point. CPAP (continuous positive airways pressure) is the treatment both boys were receiving now that they were off the ventilators, and it was a step towards breathing on their own. Whilst the nurse in charge was pleased at this progress of Tom's, I remember my heart sinking as I thought it was too long. This lady was the expert, and I was the Mum after all. I brushed aside my feelings of concern and put it down to me being a little OTT and worrying unnecessarily.

My gut didn't feel right and if I'm being completely honest, I did want to go back to the hospital. We had already agreed we would go to our friend's house to watch the football as England were playing. I knew Andy wanted to go as he's a massive football fan. I swallowed up my concerns and went. To this day I regret that decision.

We only went over for a couple of hours but because we had been shopping before, we had probably left the boys for a good six hours. This had been the most we had ever left them during the day.

Funnily enough, another stark memory of this day was seeing our friends two boys with their matching England bibs on. They were only three months and six weeks older than Charlie and Tom, but they couldn't have looked any different to our boys. They were all chubby cheeks and smiles wearing proper baby clothes!

We got back to SCBU around 6ish to find chaos in the boys' room. The sister I had spoken to on the phone looked very frantic and told us she was just about to call us. There were three or so doctors and nurses surrounding Tom's incubator. The sight of him was one I will never forget. His tummy was so big and distended, like he was one of the poor children in Ethiopia, and he was continually crying and looked extremely distressed. I popped my finger to his little hand, and he grasped it and kept squeezing it in pain. One of the doctors told me that he had suspected NEC, and they would need to pop him back onto the ventilator to give him a rest whilst they investigated next steps. I broke down there and then. Andy couldn't understand my distress. As far as he was concerned the doctors were on it and were going to treat him. Like everything in life, I had read up a lot on various different things that can go wrong for premature babies. NEC stands for Necrotising Enterocolitis and occurs when tissue in the bowel becomes inflamed. I knew it was serious. They ushered us out of the room as a locum doctor went about putting Tom back onto the ventilator. He didn't seem very confident in what he was doing which in turn didn't really help the situation. There was talk about potentially moving him urgently to the The Children's Hospital, but they were going to call the consultant in from home to come and help.

The boy's consultant was a gorgeous human being called Dr. El-Shimy. He was the kindest, most caring and patient man ever and I was relieved that he would be coming in to try and help. We were ushered into the family room where we were asked to wait. I remember bursting into tears and started to pray like the most devout nun ever. I'll never forget when Dr. El-Shimy came to talk to us and he calmly explained that he wasn't going to waste time waiting to get any results back, he was going to treat Tom straight away for NEC. He calmly told us that the worst-case scenario was that he may need surgery at The Children's Hospital. I remember telling him how unhappy we were with the care that Tom had received. How there were issues with his bedding being sullied and not correctly sanitised. I could kick myself now.......why was I telling him these things? Why was I wasting his time moaning about - in comparison - trivial things when he could have been in with Tom treating him? Clear as day I remember asking him to do everything he could to help our boy.

We were left to wait for what seemed like hours but in reality, it was more like 30/45 minutes when a new nurse came rushing into the room to talk to us. For some reason I thought we must have done something to offend or upset her as she seemed very brusque with us. Looking back, it was more likely that she was stressed. She told us that Dr. El-Shimmy had asked her to come and tell us that Tom kept "going off" and he was doing his absolute best for him. I had never heard this expression and I had no idea what she meant. Some 10-15 minutes later he came back in to tell us that Tom was dying, that he had already given him two shots of adrenaline, and that he would try one more time. I remember clinging to him and begging him to save our boy. Andy and I then cried together and just clung to each other to wait. I think at this point I already knew but didn't dare believe what was happening. It felt like the longest time ever waiting for him to return, I actually heard his shoes clicking along the corridor as he approached the door. They were slow and hesitant, and I just knew.

Andy and I clung to each other after Dr. El-Shimy came to tell us the fateful news. I can be quite a reserved person when I'm upset or in pain, even in labour I was very quiet. This was not the case after we'd been told that they had done all they could for Tom. My anguish was loud and messy. Looking back, I feel very sorry for the family that were in the adjoining room. They were in the overnight room that you go in when you get ready to take your baby home. I felt so sorry for them as they must have heard our distress.

The nurses asked us if we wanted to bathe Tom and I still to this day regret declining. We held Tom and all I can remember saying to him again and again was how sorry I was. Sorry that I had brought him into this world in the first place where all he had felt was pain. The rest of the evening was a bit of a blur. Andy had the unthinkable job of calling our friends and family. Both sets of grandparents came up to see us as we held Charlie close to us. One of the nurses that we had got close to and was on shift whilst this all happened had to leave work as she was so distressed herself. After eventually driving home, Andy and I went to bed and cried together.

Chapter 10

The next few days were some of the hardest and darkest days yet. The hospital was amazing, they took hand and footprints, and some of Tom's hair for us to keep. The one thing I remember vividly, was sitting down with the funeral director as she asked us questions like whether we would want a burial or cremation and what kind of coffin we would want for our little boy. All questions that I had no idea on where to start. Another memory that sticks in my mind is the one that I had when calling the funeral directors to ask what Tom would be wearing. The person that answered the phone gave me the stock reply of a white shirt and black tie. I was mortified and put the phone down. I could think of nothing worse. To be dressed as an old man that had had a full life of memories was unthinkable. They called me back after realising their mistake. Of course, looking back now I can totally understand that they had given me a stock answer without checking the age of the deceased. I guess two-month-old babies dying is thankfully not a common thing. All of it was so unbelievably surreal, as if it was happening to someone else. Andy's parents very kindly bought us a family plot as we felt we wanted to have somewhere to visit. Somewhere we could take our family to visit to remember him. The days and weeks that followed were foggy, with just one or two moments of clarity. The overriding emotion I had was fear, fear that Charlie would be taken from us too. I'll never forget the one day that I voiced my concerns for Charlie to his consultant. I was hoping for him to reassure me that I didn't need to be concerned but he very honestly told me that he shared my concerns too. It was for this reason that he was personally checking on Charlie every day, measuring his tummy to ensure there was no growth there. Like anyone that goes through grief I completely lost my appetite. It was only the fact that I was breastfeeding that kept me going with the reminder that I needed to eat to keep my energy up. The last thing I wanted was for my milk to dry up. The sadness that followed was unreal when I was still producing enough for two babies. I ended up freezing my milk so that I could continue for the day that Charlie would come home.

Tom's funeral came round some three weeks later. It was a beautiful sunny day, and our church was packed not only with our friends and family, but also doctors and nurses that had cared for Tom both at The Women's Hospital, as well as Good Hope. Both Andy and I wrote a eulogy for Tom and here below is mine:

No more wires
No more tubes
No more bleeping machines
No more pain

You now have peace Tom and I know that you have passed on your strength to Charlie.

Every time Charlie makes us proud by learning to walk or ride his bike. When he starts school or gets his first job, we know you will be looking down with a smile upon your face as you are still with him every step of the way.

I then read the below poem by Karen White:

If tears could build a staircase
And memories were a lane
I would walk right up to heaven and bring you home again

No farewell words were spoken
No time to say goodbye
You were gone before I knew it
And only God knows why

It was one of the hardest things I have ever had to do but I felt it was the one thing I could do for our boy.
We went straight to the cemetery to bury his coffin and after I threw the first rose onto his coffin all I wanted to do was climb in with him. This was our final goodbye after not even having the chance to get to know him, to bring him home and make memories with him as he grew. We didn't have a

wake as all we wanted to do was to go straight up to the hospital to be with Charlie.

Chapter 11

The following days that followed, Charlie just grew and grew. He became a "proper" baby right before our eyes. We were allowed to hold him continually as up until this point it had been very much restricted to holding them for only five minutes at a time as it would tire them out. More and more of the wires and tubes were disappearing and we now could see his beautiful face. He would begin to respond to our voices, open his eyes and look at us. At the Women's Hospital, we had been allowed to have friends and family come and visit the boys. As long as there were no more than two at a time. I am forever grateful for this as we do have friends and family that got to meet Tom. I quite often cannot believe that we had twins, and it is the very fact that a handful of close friends and family met Tom which helped keep his memory alive. By comparison at Good Hope, it was only grandparents that were allowed to come and visit. This was hard but actually it gave us space to just spend time with our boys. I had only ever held both boys together once during this whole time and for that I am so unbelievably grateful. It was only five minutes, but I still remember the feeling of complete happiness and contentment of being able to hold them both.

A new Mum came into the unit around five days after Tom had died and she innocently asked me whether I'd had a boy or a girl. I remember bursting into tears as I had no idea how to answer that. Even now, it's one of the questions I struggle with. To just tell people that we have two boys feels unthinkable as I can't not mention Tom. Yet the alternative of telling the truth is equally awful. The question of how many children you have is usually asked when you are just meeting someone. To then tell them one of your children has died is not what they are expecting. I usually have to gauge it depending on the circumstances. I try my very best to say that I have just two boys now. 99% of the time, people don't pick up on the exact words I say and that is what I want. If we develop a friendship further down the road then that's the time to tell them more and not when we are standing in the middle of a supermarket.

Andy and I were devastated and in deep shock as it all happened so very quickly. I look back and realise that I very quickly transferred any grief onto concern for Charlie. It was my coping strategy.

It's a unique position to be in when you lose an identical twin. We have always felt ourselves so very fortunate to have a daily reminder of what Tom most probably would have looked like. I cannot imagine the pain of losing a baby and having all this love and nowhere for the love to go. To come home without a baby is unthinkable. For us we have a daily reminder of Tom and for that we are so incredibly lucky. There is a sadness to each of Charlie's milestones and achievements. Whether it was him first walking, riding a bike, or going to school. Every single milestone, I have shed tears for the little boy that should be walking beside his brother. As time goes on, you'd imagine that this feeling lessens or becomes easier to manage. The truth is, we don't want to let go, we don't want to get better. If that was to happen it would feel as if Tom had never happened. I am quite sure that when Charlie goes off to university, meets his life partner and (hopefully) has his own family we will be thinking of Tom. Right from the start we have made sure that Tom's memory is very much the fabric of our family life. We never wanted his passing to be something that's whispered behind closed doors as if it was something to be ashamed of. Because we have always talked openly about Tom, both our boys have mirrored this (we went on to have another beautiful boy Louie) After a friend bought a star for us in Tom's name, we decided to talk about Tom as if he was in the sky looking down at us. This nightly ritual was something we did with the boys from a very young age. As kids do have an uncanny knack of saying the wrong thing, or the right thing at the wrong time this came to bite me on the bum one busy school morning……

Neither of the boys were feeling too enthusiastic about school so I reminded them we were visiting a soft play after school to entice them to get ready. Louie innocently asked if Tom had ever been to the same soft play.

Before I had a chance to draw breath, Charlie exclaimed “Of course he’s never been, how could he when he died in hospital before he even could come home!”

This brought a tear to my eye as it was a stark reminder of the fact that we never did get to bring Tom home. I didn’t, however, have the time to wallow in these thoughts as time was cracking on and we had to get ready for school. I replied, “Yes that’s right Charlie, let’s go downstairs then!”

Charlie had just tried to do the big brother thing and put Louie in his place. Little did he realise how much his comment had brought home the fact that Tom was taken from us far too early.

Chapter 12

We eventually took Charlie home after over three months of being in special care. As you can imagine it was a massively bittersweet moment for us, as we popped him into his car seat (he looked tiny!!) knowing that it should have been two car seats with our beautiful Tom coming home too. There were many tears from us and from the nurses! Whilst we were overjoyed to bring our boy home it was also terrifying. We had only ever known him to be wired up to machines that kept him in check. We were used to him having his temperature taken on an hourly basis to alert us of any incoming infections. He weighed less than 4 lbs coming home at 12 weeks of age. He was tiny and still very vulnerable. I'm so sorry to all our family and friends that came to visit as we made you sanitise your hands before coming into the house! I'll never forget when a friend called me up to tell me about the arrival of one of our friend's babies. She told me what the baby weighed, and I put the phone down on her. I couldn't cope with this news! It sounds ridiculous now when I think about it so many years later. The truth was I was pregnant at the same time as our friend. Our due dates were only a month apart and whilst Charlie was four months old at this stage, her new-born weighed more than he did. It sounds so irrational now, but I just felt such a failure as a mum. It didn't help that I was breastfeeding Charlie and was his sole nutrition. Other than having an apnoea monitor whilst Charlie slept, we tried our best to have a normal life as possible.

There were many magical moments as we witnessed our boy growing, but there were many moments of angst and worry too. We were watching Charlie like a hawk as we were aware of so many issues that could arise after him being born so early. It didn't help that we were surrounded by friends who had babies at the same time that were full term, were thriving and looked and behaved so differently. Charlie had reflux and was on a whole host of meds. As I was still feeding him myself, I'd hold him upright for a good 30 minutes before setting him down on a raised Moses basket. As I was feeding him every two hours it would seem that just as I was going back to sleep, he'd rise again. Feeding a baby that's so small it's all about the little and often schedule! This was one thing I did have in common with my friends as most of our conversations were about how much we'd been up in the night and how little sleep we'd had! Charlie had a few ongoing health concerns from a possible hydrocephalus in his brain (excess fluid in the brain), as well as surgery on his one testicle, to grommets being fitted. He had a lot of issues with his bowels that plagued him for many a year, but all of these things were minor in our head as we had him home!!!

Whilst my maternity had started the day our boys were born, I was incredibly lucky that I was able to take off over a year with Charlie. I had saved enough to be able to still have a small amount of money each month as I could think of nothing worse than asking Andy to pay for a new lipstick! I had accrued some holiday which I tagged onto the end too. As my maternity was coming to an end, I had this growing fear of knowing that I would have to return to work and put him into nursery. How could I do this? How could I entrust someone else to care for our baby like we did? How could I return to work after so much had happened to us? I had completely changed as a person. None of my priorities were the same as before. How could I care about SLA's, margins and business performance when we had lost our child and we'd gone through all we had? This is something that millions of people go through. It is so hard to go back into work mode, with the commute, the meetings, the juggle and the struggle. The overwhelming tiredness when you pick up your children and have to start again. I remember telling Andy that I wasn't sure if I could do it. All I wanted to do was to stay at home with Charlie. If he had said at that point that it was ok, we would survive on his salary, I would have snatched his hand off. As I write this today, I am SO GLAD he didn't! I have nothing against anyone that decides to do this, in fact I have so much admiration for them; I think it's an incredibly difficult thing to do. I am fiercely independent, and I do wonder if this is because of how I'm set up, was I born this way or is it because of my circumstances and the fact that I left home young? Either way I'm so glad I was brave and continued with my job. It was hard, so incredibly hard. We had secured a space for Charlie at a nursery where a friend was manager, and I knew she would keep a close eye on our boy.

I found the days very long and the battle of pretending that I cared about the business side of things was hard.
As it had taken us a while to conceive, we decided to not take precautions and were fully expecting another pregnancy to take another 12 months at least. We were wrong…….I'd not been back to work for a full month before finding out we were pregnant. To say we were surprised doesn't cut it. The only reason I took a pregnancy test was because we were going to Nice for my 30th and I thought I'd better check before a weekend of drinking! I was stunned……especially after it had taken us so long with our first pregnancy. I guess the body does know what it's doing once it's done it before!

Chapter 13

To say I felt like I was a ticking time bomb was the understatement of the year. Were we expecting twins again? (I had secretly hoped we were, so that I could try and get it right this time and go all the way) I felt a real mix of disappointment and relief to find out it was just one single baby. I contacted Dr El-Shimy to find out where would be best for my care and straight away he encouraged me to go to The Birmingham Women's. I wasn't sure how I felt going back there. We had so many memories of Charlie and Tom there. Even to this day, some 17 years later, I feel so much sadness when I go there as it was the one place we still had hope that we may, just may, be able to take our boys both home.

To my absolute delight I passed the 25-week mark, and it was only at this point that I began to breathe properly. I actually had felt like I was holding my breath up until this point! I found it a challenge to work for three full days and commute into the city each day. I used to come home after collecting Charlie and lie down in his room as he played around me as I was so exhausted.

I got to 30 weeks this time when I went into labour. I vividly remember having a small bleed like I had the first time and telling Andy that I wasn't sure if I was in labour, but it might be a good idea to get to hospital to be sure. Imagine - It's the 2nd of January, the first working day after New Year and we are driving into the city centre at peak time of 8AM! After being in the car for five minutes or so I realised I was in fact in labour and my contractions were five minutes apart. As calmly as I could I told Andy this as he was navigating his way through the horrendous traffic.

We arrived at the hospital to be whisked into the triage room. As the midwife was examining me, I got quite agitated as I knew I was in labour, and I knew that I'd need the steroids to help my baby have any chance of surviving.

SCBU came down to see me as I was in labour to tell me that they weren't worried about a 30 week-er and even though we'd had a traumatic experience the first time round it wouldn't necessarily be the same with this baby. After being in labour for a few hours, they had managed to slow things down but as I reached 9 cm they were concerned. I had placenta previa whereby the placenta is blocking the cervix but more worryingly I had a prolapsed cord. This meant that our baby's oxygen could be compromised. A doctor hurriedly pushed a consent form my way to agree to an emergency c-section. I irrationally refused as I'd got this far without any epidural and wanted to be as natural as possible. Needless to say, I came to my senses and was rushed into theatre.

I remember when the anaesthetist was putting the epidural in that I heard a sound that resembled cymbals clashing loudly in my ears. What I didn't realise was, this was me fainting as they were trying to put the needle in. I remember the nurse calling my name from what felt like a great distance and kind of coming to. I was just so exhausted and overwhelmed, I guess. Fast forward a short time later and our Louie-Lou arrived into the world. I just needed to hear him cry to know that he was ok.....I waited and I waited but heard nothing. My anxiety skyrocketed. I couldn't see what was happening as there was a barrier in front of me where the doctors were working on sewing me up. I later found out that Louie's APGAR (the evaluation of a baby's health when they are first born) score was less than either Charlie or Tom's was even though they were born five weeks earlier than him. I guess this shows the reason why he had to be born so quickly. The placenta previa and prolapsed cord could quite easily have been a deadly combination. I am so thankful that this wasn't the case, but I guess it was a pretty traumatic birth for Louie.

Once they had stabilised him, they showed me his little face all swaddled up for all of about 20 seconds as they needed to ventilate him. My very first thought was how much he looked like Tom. This is no surprise I guess as they were brothers, but he looked so much like the last time I had seen

Tom it took my breath away. Tom was corrected at the age of 33 weeks (as he was born @ 25 weeks and died when he was 8 weeks old) and here was Louie born @ 30 weeks; so they were at a very similar weight and stage of development.

It cut me up a lot.....I couldn't believe how alike they were.

They wheeled me into recovery, and I burst into tears as I watched another couple have cuddles and kisses with their newborn. We'd never had this with Charlie and Tom. We'd had to wait 10 days to have our first hold with Charlie and two weeks with Tom. Even then it was extremely sterile as they had so many wires, tubes, and a face mask. Plenty of machines bleeping and scaring the hell out of us. Still extremely precious memories but just not ever what I had envisaged. I had clung onto a fragile hope that it would be different with Louie. That we'd get to do it the right way. So many times, I've heard others correct me and tell me that there isn't a right way and I know that's true. For me, it's such a pivotal moment after carrying your baby for so long that you get to see them and hold them and have that precious skin to skin time. If I'm completely honest I still struggle now 17 years later when the subject of labour comes up. It's a subject that many women want and need to talk about. The number of times I've heard others say that they didn't get to hold their baby for 30 minutes or even an hour and how difficult it was. I try so very hard to put myself in their shoes to understand how that would have felt. They don't need me telling them to try and wait two weeks for a hold! I quite often find it easier to say nothing at all because our experiences would take over the evening and completely change the tone of the night. We have done it once or twice and I personally have regretted it as it does seem very selfish and only when I see other's eyes widen in shock or darken with pity do I realise we've gone into too much detail.

Chapter 14

I was transferred to the maternity ward whilst Louie was in SCBU and whilst I was put into a room of my own it was still difficult. Difficult because I was surrounded by other mums and their new-borns. A stark reminder that Louie was downstairs and needing intervention. Because I'd given birth at 30 weeks, I hadn't really gained a lot of weight and with no baby in tow I'm sure some of the mums wondered what on earth I was doing there! I told myself that I was lucky as I was getting some sleep, unlike the other mums, and Louie was in the best place. The medics were right, and Louie didn't have any issues at all, he seemed very happy in his little incubator and was super well behaved. I wish I could have said the same for me! I was in a lot of pain in my stomach and couldn't wee! Every time they took the catheter out, I couldn't pass urine naturally and was nearly passing out in pain. At one point I'd gone downstairs to SCBU to check on Louie and they'd had to send me back in a wheelchair as I had a funny turn. The consultant that had been looking after me during my pregnancy was brilliant and very conscientious. He had arranged an internal scan to see if he could see anything amiss but there didn't appear to be anything wrong. It was after he suggested that it was possible to go home with the catheter still in that my sister-in-law suggested I request a CT to just have a proper look at my tummy. I am eternally grateful to Liz for this as it doesn't bear thinking about what would have happened if I hadn't asked for the scan.

I remember being in SCBU with Louie when a nurse came to tell me that my consultant had requested that I go back up to the ward as a matter of urgency. When I went back up, he was waiting for me in my room and told me he was really sorry, but I was right to have asked for the scan as they'd found a problem. There was an obstruction in my bowel. He told me that it was very serious, and they would need to operate. To be completely honest my initial reaction was one of relief. Thank goodness they'd found something and that I wasn't making things up! Both of my close friends had had caesareans and bounced back remarkably well, coming home just a few days later. I'd always looked after myself, eating healthily, and exercising has always been a big part of my life. I just couldn't understand why I had struggled to recover. This was my answer and to be totally honest I don't think I realised the magnitude of the problem at first. They tried to operate on me by going in internally and I remember being in theatre before they knocked me out pleading with my eyes to the consultant to sort me out. Alas it wasn't to be.

I ended up being transferred to the Q.E to have major abdominal surgery. By this point I was vomiting lurid bright green stuff and was in a whole world of pain. The night before they operated on me the surgeon came to see me. He explained that he would need to make an eight-inch vertical incision into my abdomen. They would un-pick all of the adhesions and there was a chance that I would end up with a stoma. This was only if they needed to take any of my bowel away, but they wouldn't know if this was the case until they opened me up. He told me that I would go straight into intensive care afterwards where they would keep me under a close eye. It would then take many weeks to build up my strength again. After telling me all of this, he asked me if I was ok about it all? I remember replying that I was fine with it all, it was in fact his face and tone being so serious that worried me. He told me that it was major surgery he was undertaking with me and that he didn't like to cut anyone open, leaving such a large scar on someone so young. He added that because it was major surgery, I'd be under for at least four hours and, like any surgery, it had its risks.

Weirdly enough I don't remember being particularly worried about the surgery. I just wanted to be free from pain. By this point I had several drains attached to me, my loyal catheter, hooked up to a drip as well as a NG (Nasogastric) tube. If you've ever had an NG tube, you will know that it is not a nice experience. The tube looks huge, and you can't quite believe that they are going to shove it up your nose. The first time anyone tried to do it had been a student nurse and let's just say it was not successful and a very uncomfortable process. It goes into your nose and then into the back of your throat all the way down to your stomach. They put one in to help you stop being sick and will aspirate it throughout the day. By this point I now looked pregnant again as my stomach had swelled to such a degree. I remember a particularly low point when I asked if Louie could come up to see me as I was now too poorly to get out of bed to see him. They wheeled him up and within five minutes I was so ill that he had to be sent back to special care. I felt so helpless and the worst new mummy in the world. How could we bond with each other if we never saw each other? Was it not bad enough that I couldn't keep him in me long enough like other babies, that now I couldn't even feed him myself and cuddle him like every other new mum? Did he even know who I was? A very kind nurse sat with me and talked to me about how I was feeling, and I remember telling her that my coping strategy was not to think about my boys too much. This may sound cold hearted or callous to many, but it was honestly taking up so much of my energy to keep my spirits up whilst I was feeling so poorly that I quite literally couldn't afford to have the weight of the emotions of missing my boys. I realise now that this is how we compartmentalise our feelings and it was one of my biggest lessons on how to cope. I have since used this skill many, many times throughout my life to get through whatever hurdles are thrown at me.

Chapter 15

I had my surgery two weeks after having Louie. I have a lasting memory of asking my mum and friends to make sure they looked after Andy and the boys if I didn't make it. It sounds very melodramatic as I write this now some 15 years later, but I felt like I'd been a cat with nine lives; I'd been through so much in my life so far and was conscious that my luck may be running out. I was in theatre for over four hours and woke up feeling very thirsty.....it feels so unfair that you're not allowed to drink after surgery. I was even limited to how many sponge lollipops I was allowed to suck on! The first question I asked was whether they'd had to fit a colostomy bag and I was so very relieved that they hadn't. The operation had been successful and now I just needed to recover. I was wheeled up to intensive care for my next chapter.

Memories of intensive care are pretty distinct. I remember being looked after by an amazing nurse who washed my hair (in the bed) and was the kindest soul I'd ever met. She never left my bedside as you receive 121 care there. I was in a world of pain after the surgery. This felt worse than the pain I had pre-surgery. I was on self-administering morphine where you push a button to get relief. I was hooked up to a heart machine that checked on my breathing; that really scared me! The nurse had asked Andy to bring in some photos of me and my family to help comfort me. As she arranged them on a wall within my view she commented on one photo, asking if the person in the photo was my sister.......turns out it was a photo of me with Charlie. I had changed so dramatically, partly because of how much weight I had lost, that I looked nothing like the "normal, healthy" version of me before being so poorly. (I'm sure a massive part of this is the fact that I look like a zombie without make-up!) This was a bit of a shock for both her and for us.

The following days and weeks were a bit of a blur as I slept most of it and always felt very tired when visitors came to see me. I worked my way down to HDU (High Dependency Unit) and then eventually back to the regular maternity ward. I'd now been in hospital for over a month and had lost more of my tubes, drains and drips, but was really struggling to eat. I had a room full of snacks and treats but I just couldn't eat anything. It was such an alien feeling for me as I'd always enjoyed my food so very much. I'd never really understood when people can't just put food inside their mouths, even if just for fuel. I had begun to gain an insight into the dark world of eating disorders. Andy would come and see me and munch on cookies and I'd watch him with fascination as I just couldn't do it. I had a rather sobering chat with my consultant on a particular Saturday morning. He'd come in from home to see me as he was worried about me. He told me in no uncertain words that if I hadn't been able to eat over the weekend on Monday, he would need to get the eating disorder team involved. This horrified me and was the jolt I needed. I distinctly remember having a photo of Andy and the boys in front of me as I told myself to sip 3 spoons of soup. I don't know whether to laugh or cry as I write this as it's so far removed from anything I am today or was back then. I adore food, all food and I can't believe I was struggling so much that I had to give myself goals of eating a few spoonsful of soup. The midwives were amazing and said that whatever I fancied, the cook from downstairs would make me! How lovely and caring is that? Andy ended up going off to get me food from M&S that the midwives kept for me in their fridge. I'm very much of a goal driven kind of girl and I gave myself little goals each day of how much I'd need to eat increasing bit by bit. Having the photo of my family in front of me gave me the inspiration to keep going.

Whilst still incredibly weak, I began to build up small reserves of energy and a lot of this was helped by the fortify drinks I was instructed to drink. I had to consume three or four of these a day and I found even these difficult to stomach. At this point I hadn't seen Charlie properly for a couple of weeks and Andy was coming to visit. We decided it would be a good idea if I played with Charlie in the playroom attached to SCBU whilst Andy went to see Louie. I was desperate to see Charlie, I had missed him terribly and couldn't wait to have big cuddles and kisses with him. It ended up being a complete disaster. As soon as Andy dropped him off in the playroom with me, Charlie went running after him as he didn't want to be left with me. I was heartbroken. He wasn't allowed in the room where Andy and Louie were due to cross infection. I led him back to me kicking and screaming and closed the door so that he couldn't run out again. He beat on the door to be let out. I was devastated......all I wanted was to see my boy and shower him with love. He cried his eyes out as he didn't want to be with me. This was an extremely low point for me that I will never forget. Looking back, I can completely understand why he had reacted like this. In his mind I had deserted him, and Andy was his unwavering constant. He didn't want to be rejected by me again as in his little mind that is what I had done. He was only 20 months old.

This episode gave me the push I needed. I needed to get home and get back to being a wife and Mum. I ended up coming home five weeks after giving birth to Louie. I was at home for a week before Louie came home and that's when the fun really started!

Chapter 16

Louie came home at six weeks of age, a healthy 5Lbs in weight although he still looked very small. I couldn't believe how well he had done and the medics were spot on.....he needed no intervention. It was almost as if he knew how poorly I had been and didn't want to cause any drama himself. He came home the same day that my god-daughter Ruby was born. We marvelled at how Louie was six weeks older yet weighed less than Ruby. His due date had been 10th March, so I guess he had some catching up to do! We probably looked like quite an unusual pair, as even though I had started to gain some weight, I certainly didn't look a healthy weight, let alone as if I'd just given birth. Louie looked like a very small newborn when he came home, and I remember strangers remarking upon it. I found it too difficult to explain and quite frankly didn't want to explain our whole sorry story whilst standing in a supermarket or soft play so would just reply that I'd been poorly that's all.

Looking back at these times I have mixed emotions. My dad flew over from Canada to see us which was amazing. I was so unbelievably thankful for finally coming home and for how healthy Louie was. Charlie was still extremely jealous and quite difficult. I've since read up about the emotions that children can go through. In his little mind his mummy had left him, she wasn't to be trusted and was no longer his everything. To further compound this, a new baby had come home that was taking up my time, love and attention. I read that the strength of emotion he felt was similar to how a woman may feel if her husband brings another wife home to live with them! Whilst he was 20 months old, he was still very under-developed. He had not long been walking and wasn't really talking. He understood everything and certainly had a few words ("'No" being his favourite!)

When the health visitor came to visit us and weigh Louie, I asked her to assess Charlie. She said that he was developmentally like a 15-month-old. The reason I'm explaining this is because the gap between them felt quite small. I totally understand Charlie's angst and if I'm honest because Louie was such a good baby, he quite often had to wait whilst I was tending to Charlie. Was this a mistake that I made? Quite possibly. But if I'm completely honest I was operating on survival mode and just getting through each day. I found life incredibly hard. Andy was pretty much out of the house 7AM to 7PM. I couldn't leave Charlie and Louie in the same room for fear of what Charlie would do to Louie. I found it far easier to run myself ragged by being busy and out of the house as much as possible to keep everyone distracted. Having Charlie at nursery for two days a week was my absolute Godsend. I remember feeling so guilty for feeling this way, but I just found life so very, very hard. I'm eternally grateful for my friends. They had children of similar ages and were great at organising days out, playgroups to go to, and just generally keeping the kids busy and happy. My closest friends all had their kids at the same nursery and were able to do afternoons there and I do remember feeling quite lonely when they went off to work in the afternoons. Do I wish that I had done it differently? Partly, I guess. I never had one day when I stayed at home in my pjs and just spent time with my boys. They may have relished having this time with just me? I ask myself now, did I play with them enough? Did I get down on the floor and play with their characters? I was always into games that helped their education, I loved reading with them, and we did a lot of outdoor time and swimming, but did I do enough? Did I savour those moments? I guess this pondering over parenthood is very normal and feeling guilty for how we could have done better?

By the time that Charlie was three and he was at pre-school, I was quite concerned about his behaviour and went to seek help. He was assessed both at home and at school. We also went through a programme called Triple P that is based on Positive Parenting techniques. The therapists didn't think there were any specific changes we needed to make, but Andy and I were both happy to review how we did things and try anything.

We did see small glimmers of change, but I still felt very down. I had now gone back to work and, whilst I felt it was a big struggle as I was commuting to the city centre three days a week and doing both drop off and picking up at nursery, I actually found going to work less stressful than being at home! I completely take my hat off to anyone that looks after their children full time as I didn't think it was an easy option at all. However, if Andy had said to me that it was an option to not return to work, I'd have grabbed it with both hands. I am eternally grateful that this didn't happen. Sadly, I have friends that took time out from work to focus on their family and have since struggled with their independence. The way that we manage money is very different to many others. Whilst we have our joint accounts, we also have our separate accounts. We decide on how we jointly save and pay for things, and I wouldn't have it any other way. I could never imagine being in the situation whereby I needed to ask Andy if I could get my haircut or for money to go out with my friends. Maybe the reason for this is because I left home so young and that I had to fend for myself. Maybe it was because I worked since I was 11. I don't know but it's the way I am!

Chapter 17

Going back to work had its challenges. I had left as a team manager and whilst the business had to keep me on the same grade and salary, they had struggled to find me a role on a part-time basis. Looking back, I understand how tricky this can be. The reality was that I ended up doing a job that I didn't enjoy one little bit. I had left as Training Manager, responsible for the training needs of 400+ people. I loved both the team I was in, as well as my manager. Everything had changed on my return to work some 12 months later. A huge restructure had taken place, my job had gone, and I needed to re-adjust. So much had happened to me personally each time I had returned to work. Both times I had left suddenly, both times had been an emergency situation, and I had changed so very much. The positive side of this was that because so much had happened to us as a family, these life changing experiences had given me a new perspective on life. I no longer stressed about events at work and whatever happened I always knew that there was a solution. More than once, a colleague would comment on how chilled I was in the face of adversity. To be completely blunt, when you lose a child and when you go through life saving surgery, then everything else pales into insignificance.

I had a difficult time at work after returning from maternity the second time. I felt very targeted by my manager and there were numerous incidents that made me feel very undermined and intimidated. For reasons that I didn't understand at the time, I sunk into a very dark hole of depression. I struggled to get out of bed, I felt as if my limbs were made of lead. I honestly felt as if I was swimming in treacle and the simplest of tasks felt like the biggest of challenges. I couldn't believe that I was letting this other individual's behaviour get to me to such a degree. I remember going on holiday with Andy and the boys and still feeling no joy. It's almost as if I had no emotions in me, I felt numb. It was like I was surrounded by a bubble of numbness. I sought help from a counsellor and after a few sessions he told me that he thought I was suffering from PTSD (post-traumatic stress disorder) due to the fact that I'd never grieved properly for Tom and had instead transferred that grief onto concern for Charlie. We had then fallen pregnant far quicker than I ever had imagined and then had Louie under such traumatic circumstances, I guess it was no big surprise. Whilst this person's individual behaviour towards me was not great, it didn't warrant me sinking as low as I did. I have since forgiven this person as she was going through her own difficulties. It was this during this period that my depression was triggered and I spent almost six months off working through it. I am a massive advocate of seeking help through talking to others, both in a professional capacity as well as with friends and family.

Chapter 18

If I had one wish it would be that everyone had an annual "check in" with a counsellor. This would be your opportunity to evaluate how you are doing, how you are feeling and a chance to talk to someone completely neutral. I think that counselling should be something that we do before there is a problem. This would save so much heartache and angst. It could potentially put a halt to further complex problems that are more difficult to unravel. So many people are struggling and self-soothing with drugs, alcohol, or emotional eating.

Tragically I had a second bowel obstruction some four years later. It was almost to the day as it happened on New Year's Day whilst we were away at my brother's. I woke up early with Louie and after having a slice of toast I was in instant agony. I lay on the sofa for a while but then had to hobble back to bed as I felt so much pain. The pain immobilises you and it's so difficult to catch your breath. I slept fitfully and wasn't aware of the time that passed. I do remember making my way to the bathroom and having a funny turn there. Several hours passed and I wasn't getting any better, so Andy decided to call an ambulance. At the time my brother lived in a farmhouse that wasn't the easiest to find but they did eventually! They gave me morphine and gas and air so that they could get me into the ambulance. I was so scared of going through all of the same ordeal yet again, but I couldn't afford to even think about it. I ended up staying in Hereford hospital for nearly a week until they transferred me by ambulance to the Q.E hospital. This was much closer to home and where they had operated on me before. This was hard, so very hard. Andy and the boys came home whilst I was still stuck in Hereford, and I felt isolated and alone. I was terrified of having the surgery and looking back, I was in denial for the first few days.

I had been admitted a couple of times after the first surgery with abdominal pain. My bowel had twisted but then righted itself, so I was desperately hoping it was the same thing happening again. The nurses had wanted to put a NG tube in again and I begged them to give me 24 hours to just wait and see. Part of the problem I guess was the fact that I knew what to expect, knew what was coming and I was scared. When my tummy blew up so much that I looked pregnant I knew I couldn't deny it any longer. The intensity of the pain is so very difficult to describe as there aren't any words that can really convey. It's a pain that takes your breath away. You can't talk when it's at its peak. I remember when I arrived back at the Q.E I had got through the ambulance journey ok on gas and air. Once you get back into a new hospital you must start again with explaining your story.

It was late at night, and I was in a whole world of pain. When the doctor came round, he wasn't able to give me my usual dose of morphine; it was right back to the beginning starting with my name and date of birth! There were a couple of positives to this story. The first being, I became closer to one of Louie's nursery friends that was a doctor there. Sara would come and visit me and was very kind. I guess when people see you in this kind of mess you form a bond pretty quick! Sara is one of my closest friends now some 12 years later!

The second positive thing was the fact that Andy had private medical insurance that enabled me to have my own room and there were no set visiting times. This was a Godsend as friends could come and visit me in their lunch time and it meant I could spread out having people to see me rather than all at once. I must have looked a right sight as I had all the usual drains, IV fluids and NG tube but this time I had an added extra! This was a central line that had been put in. This is a large tube that goes into my neck and down towards my chest. They put them in when they know someone needs long term medication. I hated it with a passion. Firstly, I was awake when they put it in and whilst it didn't hurt it was a bizarre feeling knowing what they were doing. Secondly it really hurt each time I moved in the wrong way. It almost felt like an electric shock each time it happened, and it was so difficult to sleep with.

Surgery happened a week or so after arriving at the Q.E but this time they had to take away a sizable portion of my bowel. Again, I was incredibly lucky because I didn't wake up with a colostomy bag and for that I am eternally grateful. Looking back, this part of my life was incredibly difficult, and of course, I have often compared it with the first time I had the bowel obstruction. I'm trying to figure out if it was any easier the second time round. It wasn't easier, it was just different with its own challenges. I have some very vivid memories. I remember waking up in the early hours not long after surgery and thinking I was back in the 1920's. I could see a nurse in an old-fashioned uniform, and I was afraid of my curtains as they billowed with the air conditioning on. I must have sounded anxious as when a nurse asked me if I was ok, I realised she was one of the consultants. She told me that she thought I was hallucinating as that can sometimes happen with the cocktail of drugs inside me. Very surreal and super frightening!

Another particularly low moment was when my mum and Andy both came to visit me at the same time. I used to ask my visitors as soon as they arrived, how long they were staying! I think I did this as I hated when anyone left and wanted to prepare myself for when they would be leaving so that it didn't come as a disappointment. Makes me feel a little sad now that I think about it as I've always been very happy in my own company so I guess I must have felt quite vulnerable. So, this particular visit was pre surgery, and I ended up ejecting bright green stuff all over myself, my bed, and my mum! It was lurid, it was awful, and it smelled so bad! I later found out that this was my own waste that had come back up via my throat as it had nowhere else to go. How vile is that? I couldn't understand why I was being so sick but apparently even meds can cause a problem.

Another particularly bad experience was when two student nurses tried to fit my NG tube. The pain was incredible and it's safe to say they were not successful…,,this was enough to put me off for life……Imagine someone trying to stick a long straw up your nose and you get the general idea!

I was, however, forever grateful that I had a private room to myself and this time I was in the new building which had far nicer surroundings. A regular part of my day was having bloods taken. My veins aren't the best and the nurses were losing any spare part of my body to pierce. They even tried to take blood from my feet towards the end. I looked a right state as I was covered in bruises, and it hurt quite a lot when they had to re-stab me at the same site multiple times. They ended up having to call someone in from another department to try and get blood out of me. I'll never forget the casual way he assumed I was a chemo patient. This was because I was black and blue with bruises and just looked so poorly. I was particularly sensitive this day as I'd heard that Louie wasn't very well, and I just felt so helpless. He was approaching his 4th birthday, and I wasn't going to be there to celebrate his special day. This broke my heart.

Chapter 19

I couldn't believe I was going to miss my little boy's birthday. I'm a "control enthusiast" in pretty much every element of my life and my boys are no exception! My mum and friends all roped in and helped Andy. I can honestly say the only way that I could cope was by blocking out the stuff that I couldn't control. I couldn't control what was going on with my boys and I also knew that anytime I thought about them I would worry. I knew that this worry wouldn't help me, it would in fact make my recovery far longer and far harder. I had to dig deep and get through this surgery as best I could. The sooner I could do this, the sooner I'd be back home with my family.
I was in hospital for around a month and again lost an awful lot of weight. This time they put me on I/V nutrition and because I knew what to expect I was able to eat very small amounts post-surgery.

After coming home, I slowly recovered and went back to work. I had been working for 12 years and our part of the business was closing. This was a very sad time, but it was the push I needed. I had a very strong sense that I needed to do something worthwhile, something more 'me'; but what?! I went to a National Franchise exhibition as I thought I could put my redundancy money to good use with the backing and support of a tried and trusted business. I had really enjoyed weaning and feeding my boys and nutrition had always been important to me. I had enjoyed Food Technology at GCSE level and I had studied Business and Finance at University. Never in a million years did I think that the two would go hand in hand years later! The other spooky thing was that whilst I was working at RBS, I had taken the decision to gain my teaching diploma. I thought this would give me options to get into teaching if I wanted to. I knew that whatever I was going to do next, it had to be around my boys. I wanted to be able to take them to school and to pick them up. I had experienced wrap-around care, and I found it a challenge! So, the fact that I had studied food, business and teaching, seemed to indicate that the stars were aligned without me realising it! It was only after chatting to a very good friend of mine about doing a franchise that she, in no uncertain terms, told me that I could do it myself! Why pay a franchise fee when I could set up by myself? I am eternally grateful to you Gem for giving me the push I needed!

It was just four months after having my second bowel surgery that I took redundancy. It coincided with my brother getting married in Thailand. I was able to treat our family for 10 days in Thailand whilst having a good think about my new baby……. Pudding and Pie. Looking back, the fact that our boys had all been born so prematurely was a monumental catalyst in my learning about all thing's nutrition. I learnt so much about baby and young children's nutrition and the effect it has on their growth and cognitive development. Here were two living examples of what good nutrition can do to help fragile babies born too soon to the strappy young men they are today.

I registered Pudding and Pie as a business in June 2012 and was given a fantastic opportunity to provide a summer workshop to my children's school. Wow, what a learning curve that was! It was brilliant as it made me realise what I needed to do……and what not to do! I set up community classes and that was rewarding but hard. It was all about numbers as I needed to balance the venue & ingredient costs with bums on seats. I really enjoyed the interaction with families and the kids were so very enthusiastic. My lucky break came when I was asked by my children's nursery to come and run a few sessions there. At the time they had a chain of 12 nurseries so that kept me super busy. I was busy building up a cookery school on a Saturday morning and had two classes back-to-back. I am forever grateful for my right arm and friend, Lisa who helped me unfailingly week after week. Lots of fun, lots of giggles but also a lot of work. The pace was quick as we needed to get our baking turned around and all ready for parents to pick up an hour later. Everything needed to be cleaned down and ready for the next class of older students. At this point I was teaching around eight classes a week. I had franchised the business with some success. I had recruited seven franchisees but, with the exception of one or two, I think most of them had misjudged how difficult it would be to start up. It's really hard work starting up as you need to be confident to knock on the doors of schools and nurseries. You must have thick skin when things inevitably don't go your way. If I could have replicated one of my franchisees Vanessa, it would have been a doddle! Vanessa shared my vision and work ethic. She had been a chef in the army so knew her food and had the discipline to go with it. Vanessa was a super hard worker, and everyone loved her. She did six years with Pudding and Pie, and I loved having her on board. Everything was going swimmingly well until 2019 when we were all hit with the pandemic, and this changed everything!

Chapter 20

I'll never forget the day when it felt like my world as I knew it came crashing down. It was a Thursday when they announced on the news that all schools would close. It was the same day that I was told I would be unable to run my cookery school or go into any of my schools and nurseries. Our boys cheered as they made the announcement on the news, and I felt like crying. I did in fact cry that night when I went to bed. I remember feeling so much anguish about the fact that I was losing all of my hard work over the past eight years it had taken me to build up my business. I'm not much of a crier, I'm far more likely to get angry these days! I might cry over something sad on the TV, but when it comes to my own life it's like I go straight into "doing mode". This was different and one of the rare times I let my guard down and cried. Even though it was something the whole world was going through at the same time, it didn't lessen the blow. If I'm being brutally honest, I wasn't too happy about homeschooling either. I can happily teach other children but when it comes to my own kids in our home with all the distractions it brings, it feels like a whole different ball game.

It was Andy that first suggested to me that I'd just need to get myself on-line. I was the person that really hated Facetime. I felt it was very stilted, the conversation never seemed to flow in the same way, and I'd get distracted with how awful I looked rather than looking at the person I was talking to! Nevertheless, I needed to do something, so I started off by running demo sessions on how to make a few simple recipes. So many families were stuck at home and after receiving so many messages like the one below, I grew in confidence as I realised how much I was helping others with bored and fed-up children:

"Billy's involvement in your cooking classes has been really positive in lots of ways. One of his favourite subjects at school is now food technology and his confidence in cooking a meal has grown. As a family, one of my favourite things is seeing the pride on his face when he carries food he has made such as his cheesecake. On Easter Sunday he received such positive compliments from everyone... These were real compliments as it was absolutely delicious. As a family we have also tried a number of dishes we never would have tried which has helped widen our teenage girls experience of flavours and tastes in food"

Certain ingredients such as flour became scarce and luckily, I had some in stock. I didn't want the fact that people couldn't get hold of ingredients to hold them back from cooking so I would leave ingredients bagged up on my porch for people to collect. For me, this showed how powerful both social media and the community we live in can be working together. It was kinda' cool how technology was working with old school values where we care about the people that live within our community. It became quite apparent that I could help lots of different people but what I didn't want to do was to financially benefit through such difficult times for many. I decided that if all proceeds could go to our local hospital, then this would be a complete WIN, WIN. I was flabbergasted by the support and interest I received. We managed to kit out a whole ward's staff room with new furniture and a fridge. This made me so happy as it felt like by doing this, we were helping so many people. It was also giving me a focus, a structure to my week. I actually ended up feeling pretty busy as I was running four classes a week as well as home-schooling. The home schooling wasn't as successful! I found it hard, particularly with Louie as he had just started secondary school. It was a steep uphill climb in terms of the quantity and level of work he was expected to complete. All of the homework was in different places with lots of workarounds. It would take us forever to figure out what needed to be done and by that time, Louie would have lost any will to do any of the work. I figured out the best way forward was going through his work the day before so that I understood it all and was in a better position to explain it. For some subjects like Maths, this meant going through an entire tutorial section and testing myself first. This would take a good hour each evening, but it definitely meant our sessions together went smoother!

After the NHS fundraiser I was approached by a local charity Acacia to run a similar event. Acacia supports families that suffer with postnatal depression and whilst this wasn't something I was ever diagnosed with, I definitely felt that I had experienced depression. For this reason, it mattered to me, the amazing work they do. I also had a few friends that worked tirelessly for the charity. We ended up running an Easter special where 100 families joined me on-line and I taught them all how to make a cream egg brownie. It was fantastic and we all raised so much money together! Over the course of 12 months or so, I ended up teaching thousands of children all over the world including throughout the UK, The Netherlands, Saudi Arabia and Australia! Never in a million years did I think I'd be as happy as I was teaching on-line as opposed to teaching in-person. I could reach so many more children and families thanks to the power of technology.

During this period of time, I ended up teaching three different lessons; one was a supper club that was predominantly for older children who could learn how to cook family meals from scratch. The second was a Saturday morning class that replaced my in-person cooking school and was for mixed ages. In this class we baked both savoury and sweet recipes. The third class was an adult's class where we made both family meals and more complex sweet dishes. I love how these classes have brought so many people together. I also loved how much they stretched me. Stretched me out of my comfort zone, learning new technologies, and facing quite often large groups of people from all over the world. They also stretched me from a practical sense as I needed to teach myself new recipes and skills. I've never made it a secret that I am self-taught. I don't have a professional chef's background, but I do have a thirst for knowledge and to learn new skills. I guess a big part of my teaching is the ability of taking any skill right back to the beginning to ensure whoever I'm teaching can learn how to grasp a new skill, right from the basics.

A big part of my learnings and business growth was coming across MIBS (Mums in Business) led by a phenomenal lady called Leona Burton. MIBS is an international group that supports women in business. I have learnt so much from Leona and her community. It is through this group that I have been encouraged to grow. I was fortunate enough to have Leona as a mentor and I truly believe she was the catalyst in helping me push my business forward. I'm so unbelievably grateful for all the support and friendships that I have made through this community. Once the pandemic was over, I met some of these ladies at my local networking groups. It was only because of the pandemic that I stopped teaching on a Saturday morning. For me, a lot of good came out of these times. Yes, it was uncertain, yes it was a massive change to our lifestyle and being able to see our family and friends. It did give me time and space to reflect on my life, what was important to me and what way I wanted to go. I will be forever thankful for all I learnt during these times.

As I sit here thinking about the journey I have travelled with Pudding and Pie, I have an overwhelming sense of gratitude for all I have experienced and achieved. To get up every single day and enjoy this thing called work I feel so very blessed. Don't get me wrong, this doesn't mean I don't work hard, as I do. If you were a fly on the wall, you would catch me working evenings and weekends a lot of the time. The point is that I adore the work that I do. I get so much satisfaction when I think about how many children I am helping, how hands-on my work is, and how fortunate I am to be able to offer this type of experience that others can enjoy. Looking back over the past few years, I have been interviewed on podcasts and radio. I have written various different articles for different publications. I have been featured in The Good Food magazine. I have delivered keynote speeches to a wide range of audiences. It is through these networks that I have worked alongside many inspirational business leaders. I adore how we can support and lift each other up and I can't explain the overwhelming sense that I can help others with my own experiences. Quite often it is other business leaders that can help me with any challenges I have as they can look at the scenario with a fresh perspective that we cannot see ourselves as we are too close to it. Only recently I was given the absolute pleasure of receiving a Women's Who award for Solopreneur of the year. This was where I had become a finalist from some 300 amazing women and then became a winner after going through a panel of judges' interview. The best bit? I feel like I am only just starting, and I have so much more inside of me to give to others.

I have evolved during these past twelve years not just as a business owner but as an individual.

I have such a strong feeling that I can help other women by sharing my story. So many other women have experienced loss, pain and trauma. I don't want them to feel that it dictates to them or stops them from achieving the very best life they deserve.

It is for this reason that I am now a motivational speaker, inspiring women from all walks of life. I don't want anyone to ever feel lonely or hindered by the pain they have encountered. I want them to feel emboldened by their experiences to build up resilience in their life.

Chapter 21

Around this same time another huge change for me came about. I gave up alcohol, initially as an experiment. An experiment that I would have with myself to see how I got on. I never wanted to make any bold statement about giving up for life as I didn't want to set myself up to fail. I'd started drinking socially from the age of around 15. My mum and dad had been very liberal and always took on the stance that they'd rather we have a little alcohol at home in a safe environment as opposed to sneaking around and hiding it like many of my friends had been brought up to do.

I'd never been that interested in it if I'm honest as it made me sick. I probably drank in the early days to get drunk and to give me confidence. Throughout my teens, I was more interested in clubbing and alcohol was not a big part of that scene. It was only after becoming friends with a group of girls - many of whom I'm lucky to say I'm still friends with now some 25+ years on - that I discovered booze. To my utter disbelief we would meet as early as 2PM on the "all-dayer" and quite often carry on until the early hours. This was all new to me, but it became the norm very quickly. We had plenty of laughs, lots of giggles and funny memories. We were quite "out there" though as a large group of girls, and a large part of our social life was around drinking. I guess it went hand in hand with the "ladette" culture that was going on at the time. After meeting Andy and then getting married, we moved onto drinking red wine with a meal or watching a film and this became my favourite tipple. I loved nothing more than going out for a bite to eat, accompanied by a glass of red.

It was in my 30's that I started to notice that my capacity for drink was becoming weaker and weaker. I'd perhaps only have a couple of ciders and a glass of wine and end up with 3-day hangovers. I tried so many different things to alleviate how bad I felt. Some of the things I tried were eating before I went out, or drinking a glass of water in-between each alcoholic drink. I even tried switching to other drinks to exclude wine, but I still had issues. At the same time, I was having a lot of problems health-wise and I wondered if it was connected. I stumbled across something called "The Alcohol Experiment" by a woman called Annie Grace. If you are reading this and considering giving up booze, I highly recommend it! It's an experiment you do with yourself to see how you feel without alcohol in your life. It encourages you to question why you drink and explores the science behind what is going on in your mind as well as the physical effects on your body. What I want to make super clear is that I'm not demonising alcohol. I know many people that enjoy a tipple, and it doesn't have a detrimental effect on their life. Unfortunately, I also know some people that have alcohol in their life, and it dictates how they live their life. I have found it fascinating how many people have questioned me on my non-drinking, they just don't understand why anyone would not drink as it's so intertwined into the fabric of their own life – especially socially.

Whilst I did the month-long experiment, I did struggle during the first few weeks. This was a 25+ years long habit that I was trying to change. My body physically felt the effects.....I felt cranky and almost as if I was experiencing cravings. You know that feeling if you're dieting and want a big fat slab of cake? I guess this may have been the sugar withdrawal from the alcohol. Once I got through those first couple of weeks, I began to feel better and better. I felt more positive, I felt more present with our boys. I felt more optimistic, positive, and full of energy. I had focussed on what I was giving up but hadn't realised how much I was gaining. I had a renewed thirst for improving myself and my own self development. I had so much energy to devote to my business and I had ideas all the time about how I could grow. I felt more patient with my family (they will probably scoff at this bit and tell me I'm still not very patient!) I could have cried with how guilty I'd felt in the past when I was hungover at the weekend. Don't get me wrong, I wasn't a big drinker, and I was never someone that could be out for hours on end. It was almost as if alcohol had become a poison to my body and I could tolerate so very little. Looking back, I cannot believe I drank for around 10 years whilst feeling like this. Why would anyone do this to themselves? It was so weak of me. During these times I have done a lot of soul searching and really invested time in me. What makes me tick, what are my strengths and weaknesses, and what can I improve upon to be the very best version of myself. I want to be an amazing mum, wife, sister, daughter, and friend.

How often do you hear the phrase "you only live once" but it was something I began to think about a lot. We only do live ONCE! We only have one life, so we really do need to live it to the max, in whichever way that makes us happy. I have such a strong sense that I was put on this earth to do something important, something that helped others and I'm still trying to figure out exactly what that looks like, but I'm determined to live life to the max! I want to travel the world, I want to try as many different experiences as possible, I want to provide the very best life that I can for my children. I'm so incredibly lucky that I get to do something every day that I enjoy, and I guess when I work at the weekend or in the evenings it doesn't feel like work for me. I enjoy my work and I'm forever grateful for that. I've experienced unfulfilling work; I've encountered boredom at work and it's one of the worst feelings ever.

Have an experiment with yourself and try it! Have you tried to have just one week off alcohol?
I hear many people say something along the lines of "I'd like to give up alcohol for a week/month but it's my son's birthday, or we have a wedding. Have you ever gone to a party without a drink? Does it concern you that you don't think you could do it without a drink? I urge you to try it……I would be lying to you if I said it's not weird at first because it is. No different to any new habit you are trying to employ. Once you get into the swing of things it's so much better. Apart from the obvious advantage that you don't have a hangover the next day, the other huge bonus is that you will remember every single minute of the night!

In my opinion, the one thing to remember is that the first few days and weeks are the hardest. Once you've got through the first couple of weeks it gets easier and easier. Focus on what you're gaining rather than the anticipation of what you (think) you are losing. I have read a lot on giving up alcohol and have added a list at the end of this book of my recommendations. Quite often these books are highly amusing as well as being brutally honest and encourage you to take a deep dive into your own reasons on why you drink.

Do I miss alcohol?
Of course, I do! Because friends have seen me not drinking now for a few years, some of them think

"I've cracked it!" I still feel like it's work in progress. Going out and having a drink has been part of my life for over 30 years now. Did it give me confidence?! Yes!
Did it give me a nice warm feeling?! Yes!
Did I enjoy getting tiddly with my husband and friends?! Yes, Yes, Yes!!
For me, the point is that whilst I still miss it, I put a higher value on how I feel without the hangovers. I liken it to being diabetic……I imagine those individuals still have moments when they like the look of a slice of cake and may look on with envy as their friend's tuck into it, enjoying every mouthful. I just know that one glass of wine will be highly likely to make me feel pretty rotten for days later and it's not worth the short-lived joy I may feel for a few hours' night out. Do I feel left out at times? Yes of course! But again, it's a short-lived moment and when I'm up in the morning, doing a workout, or writing my book rather than tossing and turning in bed with a mammoth migraine I know I've made the right decision for me.

So, if it ever crosses your mind that you don't have a healthy relationship with alcohol, or if it's just not serving you well anymore, I'd urge you to ask yourself these questions:

Why do you drink? What would you gain if you stopped drinking? What do you think will happen if you decide to stop drinking?

My recommendations if you decide to embark on the experiment are:

Write down your reason(s) for giving up alcohol.

Write down what you hope to gain.

Explain to a handful of close friends and family what you are doing, why you are doing it and how they can help you.

Clear your diary from social engagements over the first few weeks. You probably don't need the extra pressure.

Don't worry if you overeat to compensate, and definitely don't try to lose weight over the first few months. It's kind of like giving up cigarettes and you may need the crutch of sweets or nice food to get you through the toughest first few days and weeks. Any weight gain will be short term and is to be expected.

If you do the experiment for a month and love it as much as I did, you may decide to go alcohol free longer term. If this is the case, then you may want to consider some boundaries to set in place. These are things like:

Not agreeing to go out every time. Be selective on where you go and with whom. You may discover that some people are harder to be around than others.

Having a self-imposed curfew and letting friends know that you're planning to go home at X time and not to nag you about staying out if you want to go home.

I really do hope that reading my small experience helps encourage you to try it. I can only promise you that it was one of the best things I ever did for myself!

Chapter 22

So, I may have mentioned that when we were trying to conceive, I was diagnosed with polycystic ovaries. I'd had irregular periods since I was 19 but it was only picked up after we were married, and I was about 28 when trying to conceive. After I'd had the bowel surgeries, I'd had a lot of pain in my tummy and anytime that I went to the doctors about it, they thought that it was scar adhesions from all the surgery. This made sense as they had had to open me up twice and my consultant had said it can take years for the internal scar tissue to settle down. I began to make a diary of when I was in pain, whereabouts it was in my cycle, whether I'd had to take painkillers and I began to score my pain out of 10 to see if there were any patterns. I began to wonder (after quite a few years) if in fact it was unrelated to my bowels and maybe something to do with my cycle. I noticed that there was a pattern in its frequency and that my periods were becoming non-existent. I hardly bled at all; it was almost as if the less I bled the more pain I was in. Sorry if this is too much information!

I went to the sexual health GP and before she referred me, she decided to do some bloods. To my horror she did a CA125 test that came back as raised. This is the test they do to determine if there's a possibility of ovarian cancer. After doing it a second time a month or so later it was even more raised than it was in the first place! I was referred for an urgent TV scan (internal scan); I remember feeling quite nervous about this and Andy came with me. Thankfully the scan came back clear, but I had a weird sense of frustration at these results. Whilst I didn't want cancer for one moment, I still had no answers as to what on earth was going on inside of me. Was I imagining the pain? Was my mind making me feel it? What I learnt afterwards is that when the CA125 test comes back raised or above a certain "healthy range" it doesn't just mean cancer. It also can mean inflammation, that something isn't quite right. I was referred to a cancer gynae consultant and thanks to my good friend Sara was seen quickly. After an examination and lots of questions, this consultant requested for me to have an MRI to get a closer look. To my utter relief the results came back confirming I had stage IV endometriosis. I didn't know whether to laugh or cry....... finally, I had confirmation of a name for this condition that had been so debilitating. So now all I needed was the treatment and I'd be sorted.......if only it was that simple!

To anyone that's not experienced endometriosis, I'll try and explain how it feels. It kind of feels like you're carrying hot coal inside of you. The pain can shift from my stomach to my lower back and is a constant dull ache. The technical description is:

"Endometriosis is a disease in which tissue similar to the lining of the uterus, grows outside the uterus. It can cause severe pain in the pelvis and make it harder to get pregnant".
World Health Organisation March 2023

Quite often the pain can shift to the top of my legs, and I still can't believe how far the pain can travel. I've heard that this is quite normal and to do with how the nerves are attached. It's a pain that never really leaves you, a relentless nagging pain.

The good news was that there were a few different options we could try, but the bad news was they would be unable to definitely get rid of it forever. The only way that you can do this is to have a hysterectomy. The consultant told me that she would never agree to operate on me as it was too risky and not to trust anyone that said they would try. Basically, due to my bowel surgeries, my bowel is now stuck to my stomach. If a surgeon attempted to work on me, I would almost certainly lose my bowel and quite possibly not survive the surgery. This was a bitter pill for me to swallow as this bowel surgery seemed to be haunting me. However, I thought it best not to wallow on this and try the options.

The first one was to try the mini pill as this stops you from ovulating. I tried this for six months or so but it didn't make a lot of difference! The next

option was to have a coil fitted. Now……this was something I had a fair bit of trepidation about. Ok let's be honest, I was really scared about having this as I'd had one put in a while back and the pain was that intense that I let out an involuntary scream that scared both the nurse and the doctor at the time (and probably the rest of the waiting room on the other side of the door). They remarked that they'd never had a reaction like it. This was after a couple of previous attempts with various contraptions to try. Apparently, I have a posterior, far back cervix, that is very hard to reach (sorry for any males reading this!). I was pretty shaken up after the whole experience, but it was at least in.
So now I had discovered that this was the next step to try, and although I was not happy, I knew I needed to try it.

I got booked in with the Dr who was the expert in all things female and on the day of my appointment, I explained that it had been a bit of an ordeal previously. She was brilliant and said we'd go super slow and just see how it went. There was a nurse with us and off we went to a "special" room. So, I'm legs akimbo with the speculum in, when I hear what sounds like a very quiet pip squeak of a fart!!! My eyes widened with disbelief and, just as I had the thought that I must be mistaken, I heard the poor nurse murmur, "Excuse me!"

Oh, my life!!
What are the chances?
How could this happen at this specific moment? The poor nurse must have been mortified! I could not see her as she was behind my head but the Dr was in my direct line of vision.....
I just knew I could not have eye contact with her in fear of the fact that I may laugh.....God only knows what would happen then and I would be in real danger of committing the same deed myself!

Needless to say, there was no way the coil was going in. Let's just say it felt like an elephant attempting to squeeze into a mouse hole and it was not happening! I felt pretty dejected, but it was kind of the result I had been expecting. The Dr reassured me that it was possible to get the coil put in under general anaesthetic. This seemed ludicrous to me, but I had no other option.

The appointment came through and it was whilst covid was still in full swing, so off I popped to The Women's hospital for the day. All I wanted was to have this coil fitted in the hope that my endo pain would disappear. When the doctors came round to explain whether it had been possible, there was a whole team of them all looking quite sombre. My immediate thought was that it hadn't been possible to fit the coil. It turned out that it had indeed happened, but they needed to fill me in on what they had discovered whilst doing it. Almost half of my cervix had been blasted away when I'd had something called LEEP procedure when I was in my late twenties. I'd had pre-cancerous cells results from a smear test. LEEP is when the abnormal tissue is removed using a thin wire loop that is heated electrically. The aim is to remove all the abnormal cells from the surface of the cervix. The surgeon who came to see me told me the procedure appeared to have been carried out by an overzealous practitioner who had made an error of judgement and removed a large proportion of my cervix. The doctors were confused as they couldn't find any record of the procedure at their hospital. When I told them it was because I'd had it done at my local hospital, I saw a look of understanding pass over his eyes. It wasn't quite an eye roll, but it certainly was a look of, "I thought so."

I asked them if they thought this was a reason why I'd never been able to carry full term and they replied yes. They looked so serious and concerned and now I knew why. This error of judgement had caused a domino effect of catastrophic proportions. I cannot carry full term because my cervix is incompatible. This then had been the cause of all our boys fighting for their lives and of our beloved Tom losing his fight. Quite possibly, Charlie's epilepsy was caused by his prematurity and the effect of the brain damage caused by his early birth. All of the years of pain and worry came back to this one error of judgement. I now realise that I finally had an answer as to why certain things had happened. I had blamed myself for so long that I just wasn't good enough to carry our babies full term. There must be something wrong with me and now I know.

Strangely enough I didn't lay any blame on the person that had made a mistake. We all make mistakes and I'm pretty sure it wasn't done with any malice or knowledge of the heartache it would cause us. This is not to say that I wasn't heartbroken, as I was. It doesn't serve any purpose whatsoever to let my mind wander over possibilities of what could have been if this hadn't happened. Becoming bitter and twisted about it is not going to change the facts, bring back Tom, erase our pain, or delete Charlie's epilepsy; after the initial shock I realised it gave us answers and final closure.

The good news was that the coil was in, and I could hopefully gain release from the pain of endometriosis. Sadly, this wasn't the case and after almost a year of trying it I had no change in symptoms whatsoever. My last chance saloon was to go on a drug called Prostap. This stops my ovaries from working. It is whilst I'm ovulating that the pain heightens. My consultant had been cautious about putting me onto this due to the risk of osteoporosis as it can affect your bones. The drug is administered via an injection every month. It's a chemical induced menopause, so I get all the hot flushes, brain fog and mood swings associated with the change! None of this seemed significant to me though as I just wanted the pain to go away.

I couldn't believe how dramatically the change was felt. After only a week or so of having the injection, the pain had disappeared! It was like the difference between night and day. I was so happy. Finally, I was no longer in pain. I had regular appointments with the gynae team as they quizzed me on how I was feeling and whether I was coping with the menopausal side effects. To be completely honest, the hot flashes and confusion/brain fog felt so minimal compared to what I had been experiencing. I don't feel massively happy with the number of drugs I'm consuming. I have to be on HRT too, in an attempt to help with reducing any damage to my bones. I've put weight on, most significantly around my middle and the top of my legs. I know this is a big part of getting older and I know I don't have a lot to complain about. I've always taken care of myself physically with exercise being a big part of my life, and it goes without saying that good nutrition is so important to me. I guess it's the price to pay for relief from the misery that endometriosis caused. My heart goes out to each and every woman that hates the body they are in.

Chapter 23

Have you or has anyone in your family had Cancer? Chances are you have some experience. I believe it's 1 in 2 of us who will now be diagnosed with Cancer at some point in our lifetime. I am no exception. It was my mum that was diagnosed first when she was 55 years of age. She had breast cancer, and we were devastated to hear how aggressive it was. She would need to have a double mastectomy as well as aggressive chemotherapy treatment. My mum is such a strong person and is very determined. I truly believe it was her mindset that got her through this period of her life. She was adamant that it was not going to beat her but boy it put her through so very much. We felt pretty helpless watching her go through it.

There were a couple of low moments and one of these was when she lost all of her hair. Mum always moaned about her hair because it was fine, so she was always popping curlers in her hair or thickening products. To imagine her without her hair was unthinkable. I will never forget the day I first saw her without her hair and how she held me as I sobbed. The irony of this is not lost on me; my mum is consoling me! She lost her eyebrows and eyelashes, and her beloved nails became very weak and thin. My mum is someone who has always taken care of her appearance and all of these little things build up. I never heard her moan or complain, she just gritted her teeth and got on with the task ahead. I'm so incredibly proud of how she got on with this massive ordeal. I wracked my brain as to how I could help mum and I knew that she felt very nauseous a lot of the time, so I made her some ginger biscuits which she seemed to enjoy, but it just seemed so lame. I did go over now and again to have a quick clean and tidy in-between my nurseries but again it wasn't enough. Mum had said that dad was making the dinners but struggling as it had always been her that had made the family meals, so it was a big step change for dad. I went over one of the evenings to show him how to make three different meals with similar ingredients so that he could batch cook. I'm pretty sure he tried them again by himself but it's pretty hard to teach an old dog new tricks-Sorry dad - you tried your best!

Because of the fact that my aunty had had breast cancer, it was suggested to my mum that it would be a good idea if she was tested for the BRCA1 faulty gene. It is this gene that can cause breast cancer. Unfortunately, she did have the gene which meant that my siblings and I could also have it. I learnt at this point that men can also get breast cancer! I decided I wanted to know if I had it too and was tested. I'm the kind of person that just wants to know. I truly believe that knowledge is power, and I cannot deal with uncertainty. I struggle when I'm not in control or have the facts around me. I think this is one of the hardest parts of cancer as there is a lot of waiting. Waiting for results that will determine treatment, and how your life will look for the coming weeks and months. Before the test can be done you have to have counselling to help you prepare for the worst. Long story short is that the test came back negative so I could sigh with relief! I totally get why some people decide not to find out and I know that if, for example, you are looking to get a mortgage a positive result for the faulty gene can cause real problems as you have to disclose it when applying for mortgages and life assurances. My mum got through her treatment, and we were all very happy to say that she was given the all clear and could get back to some sense of normality.

Our next experience of cancer is one that we are currently living with. This one also came well and truly out of nowhere. Andy had had a cough that just didn't seem to want to go, even after having been prescribed antibiotics. After chatting with our GP, they decided to give him a chest X-ray. He had smoked in the past and both his mum and dad had had cancer. The results came back with a small mass on his chest, but they would need a CT scan to get a closer look. This was very close to Christmas, and we didn't say a word to our family or friends. We kept it to ourselves as it just wasn't the right time. We waited for what felt like forever and his CT scan date came through for the 27th of

December. Unfortunately, we had a delayed wait to find out these results as there was miscommunication between the consultant and the team that did the scan. This meant we had something like six weeks of pain waiting for the results.

You try to get on with life as best and as normally as you can, but it's so hard, it really is. The results finally came back, and we were astonished to learn that whilst the mass they had found was linked to a chest infection and there was no cancer there, they actually had found a mass in his stomach. This was completely unrelated and would never have been discovered if the body scan had not taken place. At this point we still didn't think it was cancer and I remember meeting Andy's brother and my sister in-law for dinner on the weekend prior to finding out the results. Their friend was going through a very similar journey to us but was a few months ahead in their timeline. I remember saying to my sister-in-law that my gut instinct was that it wasn't cancer and she very gently encouraged me to think about the fact that it probably was. Their friends had gone through the same timeline, with the same type of cancer, that we would shortly learn was Lymphoma. Lymphoma is a cancer that affects the lymphatic system and commonly occurs in the glands. In Andy's case it was his stomach. When we found out the news, we had both kind of readied ourselves for the result, so we weren't massively surprised. There was so much to take in with regards to next steps and treatment. We were given all of the booklets and info with a further appointment a few days later to ask the inevitable questions. I asked Andy if he wanted to go off and grab a coffee somewhere, but he said that he needed to drive to Nottingham to make a business wide announcement of structural changes. I guess this was his way of trying to get on with things, some sense of normalcy. After a hug we went our separate ways which just seemed so wrong but what he seemed to need at the time.

Andy went on to have 18 weeks' worth of chemotherapy every three weeks. Most people know someone who has had to go through this gruelling treatment and will know it really takes over your body. Andy dealt with it so incredibly well. He carried on working throughout until the last few weeks when he just felt too weak. It wasn't an immediate change; it was subtle changes that cumulatively occurred. He lost all of his hair, his eyebrows and pretty much everywhere else! All of his bones ached, and he was immensely tired. He had painful ulcers in his mouth, and he started to lose his fingernails and toenails. He soldiered on and I cannot begin to tell you how proud I am of him. It was hard to live with though. We had to be very careful about where he went and to avoid large public places. He had to change his diet as he wasn't allowed so many of the foods that we enjoyed as a family. It felt like we were back in covid times but whilst Covid was hard we were all in it together. This felt very different as all of our family and friends were able to do all of the normal things that we enjoyed so much. As I write these words I feel as if I'm claiming pity and for you to feel sorry for us. The truth is on the outside we were coping really well, and life hadn't changed that much. The reality is that we were devastated that this had happened, we were just trying our very best to soldier on and make the best of it.

One of the biggest sacrifices we had to make was cancelling our holiday to Mexico. We live for our holidays, it's the absolute highlight of each and every year. We have been very fortunate to have been to so many incredible places all over the world and the more that we go, the more we want to explore. For me, there's nothing like spending time with each other, exploring new countries, sampling new foods, and gaining new experiences. We have ridden an elephant in Thailand, scaled waterfalls, and gone ocean horseback riding in Jamaica. We have ziplined and abseiled in Mexico, ridden bikes in Central Park and we all have a hunger for more. I love every single aspect of going away; from the heat that hits you as you disembark from the plane to the new smells and culture that you get to explore. I count the days that we have remaining on every single trip and when the two weeks are up, I come back reluctantly wishing that we could have just one more week. I have to admit that the sunshine is a big factor for me. I am a bit of a sun worshipper - it feels like medicine to me. I could quite happily sit out in it for eight hours solid. I know this isn't very healthy for more than the obvious reason, but it goes even a little deeper for me. With Andy's diagnosis came the realisation that we would have to cancel our beloved family trip away. I was ashamed with regard to how hard I found this. This was only a small price to pay when Andy was going through so much. Some people don't mind not going on holiday and some people don't mind going away just to the UK. That's not me. This was the second time that Mexico had been cancelled for reasons outside of our control. We had booked Mexico pre covid and it had been cancelled when no-one was able to travel. Cancer has taught me that it's unhealthy to be so fixated on things like an annual holiday. We live for 365 days a year and it's not good for anyone to put so much emphasis on just 14 of these days. We ended up swapping our two weeks in Mexico for four nights in Brighton. Do you know what? We had an amazing time! We were blessed with fantastic weather which always helps, but we did lots. We did lots of sight-seeing, ate out, and just had a really lovely time. You cannot compare two weeks in Mexico to four nights in Brighton as it would be like comparing a steak dinner to cheese on toast (I love both!); they are just completely different. I guess you could say we made the absolute best of the situation we had found ourselves in.

Another challenging aspect of Andy's diagnosis was the boys. Because of the fact that Andy had shaved his hair on numerous occasions, it wasn't that much of a shock to see him without hair. Because of the fact that they were used to him working from home, again it wasn't a massive deal that he was home a lot. On a daily basis, I think they kind of forgot that their dad had cancer and that was hard. If you live with teenagers, you'll get this! I think a big part of this was that Andy was trying so hard to get on with life as best he could and as normally as he could. I'm not going to lie, I found it hard too. I tried my utmost to keep everyone happy and upbeat, but it was hard. My working week is pretty full-on, as physically I teach a lot and mentally have a lot to juggle.

We actually decided to go and see a therapist whilst Andy was going through his treatment. By complete coincidence our therapist had a lot of experience helping those going through the cancer journey. We both found the whole experience really helpful. We both wanted to get the most out of our boys and family life. If you've ever had teenagers, then I'm sure you'll agree it can be a challenging time. Naturally they can be quite self-centred, and combined with what we were going through, we'd experienced some challenging times.

Having this weekly time together gave us space outside of home to reflect on us, how we were and what we were going through. Fairly quickly we began to see changes emerge at home and I guess this is no coincidence. Having this time was beneficial for us both and I'm so thankful that we met Linda. Andy is a "man's man" and I think it was a big step for him to take. We hear so much talk about it's "ok to not be ok and to just be kind," but I still feel there is such a stigma surrounding mental health. I'm a firm believer that if you look after your mental health then everything else will follow suit. Life can be so tough on us all and I honestly believe that everyone has at some point in their lives the need for some help and support through counselling. If I pop my rose-tinted glasses on, then I'd love it if we all had access to an annual mental health check-up. This could be as little as just one hour to talk about where we are at, what is going on in our life and to just have someone to listen to us. Why wait to go and see someone when you are in pain or struggling? Why not look after our minds on a regular basis, giving ourselves the time to breathe and just be?

I'm a massive believer in being transparent about our lives. I totally understand why others can struggle, especially with social media images of others living their best life. It's not the whole story, it's just the bits that others want to show you. Because of this reason I decided to post about what we were going through. I'm conscious that I'm on social media a lot because of visibility within my business. This shows what my business is up to, what it's achieving, but I feel it's super important to let people know about the struggles behind this. Before I posted I showed Andy, as it mentioned him and the fact that we were seeking support. I value his opinion and he said something really interesting that I hadn't even thought about. He said that potential head teachers may see my post and then reconsider working with me if I was potentially going through mental health struggles. I totally understood this and agreed with him. It wasn't something that I had considered. I gave it some serious thought but then decided that if there were head teachers that decided to avoid me because of this, then that was certainly their prerogative, but honestly, I wasn't sure that I wanted to work with others that had this opinion. I want to work with forward thinking people. I want to be honest and transparent with everyone I meet. Life is hard for everyone regardless of what occupation they have, what their childhood was like, their status or wealth. It's really important that I work with others that have a similar outlook to me. They aren't judgmental of others or have old fashioned opinions.

After Andy went through all of his treatment we were told just before Christmas he would be ok to go on the maintenance treatment which was an injection of chemotherapy drugs every couple of months. We hugged each other with joy within the consultant's room as we couldn't believe the news. This was the best possible outcome we could have hoped for and whilst he would still have some side effects, they would be easier to manage. The most important thing would be that we could begin to get our lives back on track, begin to make plans and enjoy life again. Sadly, just a week later we were called back to go into hospital urgently as things had changed. The blood cultures had developed over Christmas and now indicated that Andy had the more aggressive type of Lymphoma, and he would not only need another course of chemotherapy but also a stem cell transplant. We were told that his treatment would take all of this year and any plans that we had wanted to make would be put on hold again. This was the day before Louie's 16th Birthday and a huge blow to us. I couldn't believe how calmly Andy took it all. Every single plan that he had made and was looking forward to was no longer possible. We had planned a fancy cruise to celebrate our 20th wedding anniversary as well as both boys finishing their GCSEs and A Levels. Andy had applied to join a golf club so that he and Louie could enjoy together. The biggest blow for me was that after not being able to go to his beloved AVFC football games for almost a year he was unable to do this for the upcoming season either. It was at this point that I cried, cried for him and cried for just how unfair it was. As I write now, Andy is currently finishing his chemotherapy and waiting to hear next steps for the stem cell transplant. Saying how proud I am of him does not convey how I feel. He has soldiered on, trying to keep life as normal as possible. He has shown how incredibly strong he is and I've been amazed at how he has kept his humour going (most of the time!!)

Chapter 24

So, I've already told you that my dad emigrated to Canada when I was 12. I loved my dad so very much and we always had long and meaningful chats over the years. I also had a lot of conflicting emotions when it came to my dad. I felt guilty because I didn't keep in contact with him as much as I could have. I'd gone to visit him when I was 16 and then 19. After that, I hadn't the money for the cost of long-haul flights as I was supporting myself through Uni and then my first few jobs didn't pay a lot. There was a gap of time from when Andy and I met before we had the boys that I may have had the money for the flights, but I was selfish. I was young and just wanted to go on holiday with our friends. As I type these words, I realise that the window of time for me being able to afford to see my dad was pretty small and I shouldn't feel guilty, but I do. After we had the boys, dad would try and call on a Sunday and would want these big chats. I'm ashamed to say I just didn't want them. I was happy to message him to see how he was and to have the occasional chat, but I was pretty exhausted with having two little boys so close together. I became frustrated by him also because he'd make comments about how the planes flew both ways and it would be nice for us to come over to see him. In the 32 years that my dad lived in Canada I saw him seven times. This seems like such a small number of times. I'm not blaming him or laying any responsibility with him. I just wished that he realised I was doing my best and that when he decided to emigrate that it was his choice. Even saying those words sounds really harsh and I don't mean to be.

My dad had recently gone through a divorce for the third time and was feeling fairly vulnerable. He had sold the family home and had moved in with family whilst he decided what he was going to do. He had bought a boat and was working on it daily. Dad was now 71 but he wasn't your regular 71-year-old man. He was very fit and active and seemed so much younger. He had a hunger for learning and loved chatting to new people. I got a call early on a Thursday morning during half term and it was my step-brother Davis. I answered his call asking him if everything was ok? I didn't even know he had my number, so it was a complete surprise. When he told me that dad had died, I was in complete shock. He had had a massive heart attack that had killed him instantly. No warning signs, no symptoms or illness. I needed to tell both my brothers and my mum which was pretty tough. It was 2021 and the pandemic was still happening. People were allowed to fly but you had to be covid free. As dad had divorced his wife it was now down to us kids to sort out his funeral and affairs. We barely knew Carrie and Davis, his step kids. Very quickly we managed to get flights booked over to Canada. We stayed with dad's cousins who were amazing! To have three complete strangers come and stay with them can't have been easy. They met us with open arms, and I will be thankful for the love and compassion that they showed us.

Our time in Canada was a bittersweet one and a whole mix of emotions. We got to experience where dad was staying, meet family we had never met before (which was incredible), we sailed on his boat and scattered his ashes which was a moment I will keep stored in my precious memory bank until the day I die myself. It was also extremely hard. We were there for only a week and had so much to do as we needed to arrange his celebration of life and pack up his apartment, all whilst feeling very emotional and jet lagged. Looking back, I think we were all in complete shock as we had been given no warning signs that dad was unwell. It's never ever going to be easy when one of our parents dies and grief is certainly something that we all have to go through in our own way. Between me and Andy we have five parents and we have now lost three of them, all in completely different circumstances. I think when someone dies suddenly it is undoubtedly the best for them. There is no suffering or pain. For me there was no goodbye. There was no time we could spend with Dad to tell him how much we loved him and how, even though we lived thousands of miles apart, he had played such an important part in creating the person I am today. Some of my traits like honesty and plain talking are down to my dad. I see elements of him in me a lot. How much I love talking to anyone from all walks of life and can literally talk the hind legs off a donkey about pretty much any subject is down to my dad (although my mum is a great conversationalist too). My brother Dean reminds me so much of my dad it's insane. His mannerisms are just like his, and I guess he still lives on in all of us in some way. I really enjoyed our time together with my two brothers. Scott, Dean and I do have a special bond as the memories of what we have experienced throughout our childhood do bring us closer together. Dean commented on the flight out to Canada, that this was most probably the only time in our lifetime that we would have time together with just the three of us and to savour it.

Dad wasn't religious and a traditional funeral would not have been what he wanted. Other than this we didn't really know dad's wishes and were navigating our way pretty blindly. The one thing I felt very strongly about was the fact that I wanted to see dad before he was cremated. This strong pull may seem strange for some. and I guess a big part of this was my own desire for acceptance and closure. I hadn't been by my dad's side as he passed, and I wanted to see him. Initially I didn't even know if this was possible as there was a couple of weeks between when he had died and when we were able to see him. Turns out it was possible, and I will be forever grateful for our time together. It was my dad's cousin's daughter that looked after dad and made all the cremation arrangements and she handled everything beautifully and with so much kindness. Even details like what dad was wearing were perfect. Dad wasn't a suit and tie kind of guy and we had arranged for him to be wearing one of his favourite jumpers. This sparked a memory for me that had been buried for over 40 years. When I was about four, my mum and dad had got dressed up to go out and I had asked who the man in the living room was as I didn't recognise my dad all suited and booted! It just wasn't dad's style - in fact he was known to have a couple of items of clothing for many a year that he would continue to wear. Clothes just weren't his thing and I guess my love for clothes was gained from my mum!

Going to see dad after he had passed was surreal. I kept expecting him to jump up and scare me with an. "only joking" and a big grin on his face. Dad was such a joker and he'd have said. "I can't believe I've had to die for you to make it over here to see me."

After going to see him and scatter his ashes on his boat it was time for his "funeral". We had all decided we wanted to say our own eulogy, to share our own memories of dad and say our goodbyes. I had done this before for Tom and knew how emotional I would be. It was really lovely to meet

some of dad's friends from both Vancouver and the island. Dad seemed to have different groups of friends from the various parts of his life. and I could most certainly resonate with this.
We still had so much to go through in terms of dad's estate and two years on, we are still figuring it out. It's not easy as we are on the other side of the world and things are so different. We not only have the time difference but also, we don't really know our step siblings. As dad had chosen both me and Davis to be joint executors, then we needed to work through it together. Whilst we did have a challenging time to get through, we did have our love and respect for our dad to guide us. We all agreed on how dad would want us to work through this together and I hope that he was proud of us for coming together. Even decisions regarding whether we would have a headstone and where it would be located took some consideration. In the end we decided to have somewhere in Canada next to our grandparents as well as a tree planted over here in the UK. Dad lived the first half of his life in the UK and the second in Canada and I know he had fond memories of both so it was fitting that we had both places to remember him.

I have now experienced grief in a number of different ways and have come to the conclusion that we all have our own ways of dealing with it. There is no right or wrong way but there is no avoiding it. I suppose if you liken it to a tall hedge

in front of you, there are a number of ways that you can work your way through the hedge to get out the other side. You can go under it, over it or through it. but you can't avoid it. You have to decide which way works best for you. No one can prepare you for the shock of losing a loved one. Friends and family can be there for you as best they can. but no-one can take away the pain. The pain of losing our baby, 17 years later I still feel disbelief, I still feel pain, pain for what was snatched from us and pain from not having a memory bank of special memories with him BUT I actually want to still feel the pain. This pain reminds me of the love for him, the fact that he did exist and is still very much part of the fabric of our family. Tom is never whispered about in hushed tones or behind closed doors. but his name is mentioned intentionally and as part of our everyday conversation. I am so thankful that we have family and friends that got to meet Tom as sometimes I have a strong sense of disbelief that he was here for a short time. It all sounds like madness I know. but I guess the fact that we never got to bring him home is a big factor in this. A phrase I heard once that has stayed with me ever since is:
"To have loved and then lost is better than to have never loved."

This is extremely powerful to me, and I have to say that I feel very close to my dad's spirit now that he has passed. I possibly think about him more since he has passed and the life lessons he has taught me, than when he was living. I can most definitely thank Tom for all he has given me as he is my drive for the dark days, my courage when I'm losing confidence and the fire in my belly for all I want to achieve.

Chapter 25

This chapter is not just for people that live with epilepsy, this is for all of the family and friends that live with the condition. I'd even go so far to say it's for anyone that lives with a condition that affects their life.

If by reading this book I help one person to feel understood and not on their own, then I will feel so incredibly happy and I will have achieved my lifetime goal. I share with you my learnings on how to best deal with living with any long-term condition. It's my belief that even adding one small habit to our everyday life can make all the difference.

I'll never forget when it was first suggested to us that Charlie may have Epilepsy. It seemed like such an alien word to us. I knew very little about it, didn't know anyone that had it, but I knew it was something major. If I'm completely honest I didn't really need the formal diagnosis as it was clear as day that it was Epilepsy. No matter, the fact still remains that it's very scary to hear the words. Charlie had both an MRI as well as an EEG to confirm his Epilepsy.

Charlie was nine when he had his first major fit whilst we were in Center Parcs.

I remember it like it was only yesterday.......

It was morning time, and we were rushing to meet family to go roller skating. Charlie was a foot or so behind me when he went hurtling to the floor and banged heavily into another visitor standing at the reception desk. Charlie was face down, so I rolled him over. I'll never forget how he looked...... He was still fitting so was jerking with his jaw in a fixed position, eyes staring. This sounds like madness now, but I actually thought he had caused himself some kind of brain damage as his features didn't look like his own. Incredibly lucky for us, there happened to be a paediatrician walking past that saw what was going on. She very calmly helped me get Charlie into the recovery position whilst staff called 999. She told me he was having a "Grand Mal Seizure" which I would later learn is also known as a "clonic tonic". I just remember putting my hand onto his chest to feel for his heartbeat. As long as I could feel his heartbeat, I knew that he was still with us. I still do this now, eight years on.

The ambulance seemed to take forever but the staff at Center Parcs put a protective shield around us which helped as we were in a very busy public reception area. We were thankful that we were with family so that they could look after Louie whilst we were whisked off to hospital to find out what on earth was going on. This was Charlie's fifth ambulance trip, little did we know he would end up clocking over 25 more on different occasions! We used to call out the paramedics every time Charlie had a fit, but we ended up making the decision that we could handle the fits ourselves. This didn't happen overnight, but we did start to grow in confidence. We noticed what was normal for Charlie. Don't get me wrong, the paramedics were invaluable in their support. They never ever made us feel that we were wasting their time and always stayed with us until Charlie fully recovered. I'm incredibly grateful for the NHS and the people within it. Very special people indeed.

So back to Centre Parcs......we were whisked off to Nottingham hospital. Charlie was very sleepy, and we have since found out that after fitting, the person is so tired that having a seizure is the equivalent of running a marathon. The doctor suggested it might be epilepsy and it felt like our world was crumbling around us. It felt like such a mammoth thing to contemplate.
What did this mean?
Would he be on medication? Could he grow out of it? How could we keep him safe? Would he die from this?

It all seemed so life changing and whilst I kept strong and upbeat around Charlie - as that's what we do - inside I was crumbling. Our boy had come so far in life. He has already overcome so many obstacles. This was the boy that had defied odds by

surviving after being born three months early. I was still in touch with other mums that had given birth later on in pregnancy - so @ 28 weeks - and their children were oxygen dependent or living with additional needs.
It was this very fact that helped us come to terms with Charlie's diagnosis. If we had been told at the time of Charlie's dangerously early birth that he would come home, he would survive but he would have epilepsy, we would have taken that gladly.

After spending the entire day at the hospital, we were discharged and came back to Center Parcs. Our family had looked after Louie all day and we were so very thankful for them.
Looking back, I think we were a little shell shocked, trying our best to take it all in. We had so many questions, but they would need to wait until we went to see the consultant back home.
Charlie had chipped his front two teeth badly which I was really upset about too. A trip to the dentist was needed!
All we wanted to do was wrap Charlie in a big bubble, look after him and keep this within the confines of our family unit.

We learnt fairly early on that Epilepsy would rear its ugly head countless times within our family life and as Charlie grew, he wouldn't always be with us. It's very tempting to keep it within the safe confines of family and friends. The problem with this is that people do need to know about this condition when you're not with your child.

I have always and still do feel like I am asking a lot for someone to have Charlie in their care. I can give them all of the advice of what to do if it happens but it's scary and it's a big responsibility. For me to say, "Just call 999," and they will help support you, I appreciate it is not an everyday occurrence. It had become quite normal for us as time went on, but I know for many people they may not have had a reason to call the emergency services and unsurprisingly this can be a big deal.

It's so very tempting to not say anything, as 99% of the time everything will be ok, and Epilepsy will not rear its ugly head. It's that 1% of time that you are gambling with. Ultimately, I feel I would be gambling with Charlie's safety, and I won't do that. If the people that are looking after Charlie are aware, then they can keep an eye on him and can leap into action should they need to. It's quite ironic that out of all of my close family and friends it's only my Mum, sister and brother-in-law that have actually witnessed him mid fit. Am I a really bad mum for wishing that others were with us when it happens? I am so very fortunate that I have some really close friends and family that want to hear blow by blow of what's happened every time it happens. They really care and have lived through every episode with me. In the past I have just wished that they could experience one seizure to understand fully. Completely selfish of me and ultimately, I know that Charlie would not want others to witness what happens. Charlie gets no warning of what is about to happen. Others talk of an aura before a seizure takes place. This helps them get themselves safe, sitting or lying down somewhere. I so wish that this was the case for Charlie. When he eventually comes round, he is extremely confused and disoriented. I feel a rush of sympathy for him, particularly if he's wound up in an ambulance or has strangers around him.

A special mention must go to two of his friends, Matt & Lorcan.

Around the age of 14, Charlie started walking to school with his mate Matt. Matt would come and pick Charlie up and they would walk until they met Lorcan and go on to school. Matt had my phone number in case of emergency. There were three different incidents of Matt calling me. The first one was when he knew something wasn't right with Charlie. He hadn't collapsed and was still walking but wasn't talking. This doesn't sound massively strange in itself but thanks to Matt's insightful and sensitive ways he knew something was up. Charlie was actually having a partial or vacant seizure which is a lot harder to spot. I rushed over to school to find Charlie in the school office. As I rubbed his back to comfort him, I realised how hot he was and encouraged him to take his blazer off. I was horrified to discover that his shirt underneath was soaked through. He told me afterwards that he felt incredibly ill but couldn't communicate. He said that he felt trapped in his own body. Whilst this is not as dramatic to see for bystanders or anyone that is with Charlie it is extremely traumatic for Charlie as he is conscious of everything but cannot alert anyone to what is going on.

The second occasion was another partial seizure where Charlie stopped chatting to his mates whilst walking to school. He ended up walking away from both boys off into a side road instead of over the main road. As they are such good lads, they followed him and called me to alert me of the situation. How many 15 or 16-year-old lads would have done this? They could have been forgiven for thinking Charlie was in a funny mood and carried on walking to school. I'm eternally grateful for these two boys - their caring and responsible attitudes.

The last incident whilst walking to school was a major one. It was raining heavily when Charlie had a seizure on the way to school. It was very public where lots of school kids from different schools were on their morning travel to school. One of his friends took their coat off and slid it under his head as Charlie was fitting on the pavement. When I got there, some of the refuse men were trying to help too. Charlie became very combative when he came round, and I've since learnt that this can happen if the person having the fit is confused or in an environment they are not sure of. I was overwhelmed with the kindness from strangers, one lady rushed back home to get a blanket for Charlie whilst another held onto him whilst I rushed back to the car to get his emergency meds. I was desperate to keep things as low key as possible. Unfortunately, a driver passing by stopped the line of traffic to offer help. Bless him - he was only trying to help but unfortunately this just meant that he had a stream of cars behind him all gawking to have a look at what was going on. I get it - I'd have been exactly the same! I ended up having to call an ambulance as I was worried about Charlie running out onto the road. He was very confused and kept trying to pull away from me. He was now 15, taller & stronger than me. All ended well as he calmed down, the paramedics checked him out, and we even had one of his teachers come and pop her head in the ambulance to see how he was!

I've always wanted to respect Charlie's privacy, he's a massively private person anyway. He doesn't like fuss and given his choice, he'd rather no-one knew about his condition. It's a fine balancing act getting it right; keeping people informed that need to know whilst respecting Charlie's wishes. I've encouraged him as he's gotten older to take responsibility for himself. So, when he went swimming, to tell the lifeguard of his condition so that they could keep an eye on him. In this day and age there are so many things that are going on in people's lives. So many health concerns, developmental or learning difficulties, I think and hope that our children are used to being surrounded by all shapes and sizes. That they are compassionate and understanding.

When Charlie was around 15, he had a particularly traumatic seizure as he was midway eating his breakfast. Because of the fact that he had no warning signs of an imminent seizure, he ended up choking mid seizure. I desperately tried to clear everything that was in his mouth, but it was virtually impossible as he kept biting me whilst he was still fitting. As Andy called 999, we weren't too sure if Charlie was actually breathing. Emergency services sent for a doctor to come out at the same time as the paramedics. Every single second seemed to stretch like minutes, every hour like days.

By the time the Paramedics arrived Charlie had stopped fitting, and I was able to clear his airway. The paramedics as usual were superb and didn't leave until Charlie had fully recovered. This particular seizure really frightened me and made me realise how incredibly vulnerable Charlie was. We were mid-way in sorting out his meds and

needed his consultant to confirm with Charlie's GP the revised dose of medication. Rather than do this, the locum doctor sent for an in-person appointment some two weeks later. This delay further frustrated me as I felt that Charlie was a ticking time bomb, and the two weeks couldn't come quick enough.
I put my hand up to admit that I was very frustrated and extremely concerned about Charlie's safety.

When we walked into Charlie's appointment to see the locum doctor, I explained why we were so concerned. Unfortunately, the doctor didn't have the bedside manner that we had experienced from BCH (Birmingham Children's Hospital) and told me that if I had been concerned, I should have taken Charlie to A&E. I was completely shocked by this response, particularly given the fact that we were mid pandemic, and it was all over the media that A&E were swamped and to avoid at all costs.

I'm a pretty calm person and like to think that I am level-headed no matter what is thrown at me. Unfortunately, I saw red, and an argument began between us. Has this ever happened to you? Something happens when it concerns your children and the inner lioness within us surfaces. I couldn't get over how shocked I was by this doctor's attitude. Surely, she could sense how stressed out I was and could have nipped it all in the bud by suggesting we start again with Charlie right at the centre of our conversation?

The final straw that broke the camel's back was when I requested that she adjust her face mask as it wasn't covering her nose and mouth……. rather than doing so she replied, "I don't need to do that actually."

I could not stand this dreadful attitude anymore and promptly walked out to seek some support.

To cut a very long story short, a mediator came into the room to discuss best ways forward. I completed an official complaint regarding the doctor's attitude. I found out later that she was leaving the position very shortly and that her attitude was not shared by the rest of the BCH team.
Considering how much involvement we've had with medics these past 16 years, I guess it's not bad that this was the only run in we've had. I look back at our time in SCBU and we really became close to the nurses and doctors that looked after our boys. This was no surprise as we were there around the clock and only going home to sleep. There was a mutual respect shared by us, the parents, and the professionals that looked after our boys and it was very much a partnership. There were different examples of where we would notice a change in one of the boys such as their colouring and when

we mentioned this to the nurse or doctor, they listened to us. In this example they tested their blood count and sure enough they needed a blood transfusion.

My advice here really is to befriend your expert whoever they are. They are only human and may make mistakes now and again especially if they are a little tired or stressed.
I look back at our experience with the locum doctor and am a little ashamed of my behaviour. Yes, she was unprofessional and rude BUT I lost sight of the fact that Charlie was in the room and didn't need to hear us squabbling. He was the reason we were there, and he was far more important than getting my point across.

Chapter 26

If you're anything like me, all you want to do is wrap your beloved in cotton wool. The mind monkeys have a field day and visit me on a daily basis.

"What if it happens whilst Charlie's walking over the road."

"What about if he's at the top of a cliff?"

"What about when he's older and can drive?"

My absolute biggest fear is water. We were told by his consultant to never leave him in a bath which Charlie is pretty cool with as he's a shower kinda' guy!

My mother's instinct would go into overdrive on a daily basis. You'd probably never see it as I try to keep it covered up. Right from the start, probably even before Charlie was diagnosed it was so very important to me that Charlie led as normal a life as possible. In fact, scrub that... as fulfilling a life as possible! After losing Tom it was a stark reminder to us, that you only get one shot at life before it could be cruelly snatched away.

When Charlie was in his last year of Junior school, he had a week-long residential trip and the school asked if I would go along on to assist. I was happy to do this, although it did come at a price as I was self-employed. Once I'd sorted out work and made arrangements back at home, I was looking forward to sharing this experience with Charlie and his friends. If you've gone through Y6 you will probably know that the year is jam packed full of exciting stuff to mark the end of primary school life. It ended up being a really difficult year for both Charlie and us.

First of all, school had been very vigilant over keeping Charlie safe during school. Part of this was that they had given him a toilet buddy. In the beginning lots of the children were happy to be his buddy but the novelty soon wore off and unfortunately Charlie had a seizure at school in the middle of his classroom. This was very public, and all the children saw it. I'm guessing this frightened them and a sad part of this was that I feel it ostracised Charlie. Combine this with his meds making him feel very down and depressed, it was catastrophic for him. He seemed to lose his way with his friends and lost his sparkle. I'll never forget the feeling of desolation on his last day. We had been invited to have a picnic with all the other families of Y6 and all the kids were running about, waving either a yearbook or shirt around to get signed. They all seemed so happy, so carefree. Charlie sat on the rug with us and told us he was just "fine" and didn't want to be with the other children. I believe that this can be the sad same experience for many children as they fly the warmth of infant school. There are a variety of reasons why, and I guess that was the same for Charlie. I certainly wouldn't pin all of the responsibility on Epilepsy, but I do believe it was a big factor.

After Charlie had attended his residential trip there was another two-night trip at the end of the year and it was proposed that the school would take them to London. I felt very strongly that it would do Charlie the world of good going without me. This would be a valuable stepping stone prior to starting secondary school. If the truth be known, I had brought Charlie up with me by his side wherever possible. The reason for this may be for a variety of reasons but you can bet your bottom dollar that his start in life, losing his brother so tragically and then the Epilepsy diagnosis are big reasons why. It was now time for me to put him first, not my own feelings, and I realised that he really didn't need me mollycoddling him!

School had asked me to go through a risk assessment with them after I declined their request to accompany Charlie for the reasons I've just outlined. I had a meeting with the head, the head of medical care, and the deputy head.
We started by running through the itinerary so that we could assess each portion of the day.

Some of the questions were around what action I would propose if Charlie had a seizure on the coach. When I responded by recommending pulling over on the hard shoulder, they were outraged that I would expect the coach driver to do this. When they asked me what action I would propose if Charlie had a seizure in the middle of London and I said to call 999, they replied that they had no idea where any hospitals in London were. This line of questioning was relentless, and I soon realised that this in actual fact was not a risk assessment but more of trying to get me to crack under pressure. I wonder whether their desired outcome was that I'd roll over and go? After what felt like a grilling for almost an hour, I'd had enough. It was nearing home time and I was picking up two additional children to my own and I was in pieces! Never have I lost my cool or become upset at school. I really did feel bullied and so incredibly upset. Needless to say, Andy called up the school and re-arranged our meeting for the following Monday, this time with him present.

In the meantime, I wrote an email to the head explaining how I felt and that we must brush our own feelings aside and put Charlie at the forefront of our minds. I also explained how overprotective I was towards Charlie after losing his twin brother. This was to explain why I wanted to be everywhere

Charlie was to make sure he was ok, but that it wasn't going to do Charlie any favours at all.
You can imagine my dismay when I didn't receive the courtesy of a reply back, made all the worse given the fact that I later learnt that the head herself was a twin. I guess I'll have to give her the benefit of the doubt on that one......

My point on all of this is that in my opinion you really do need to let your child or loved one live their life no matter how hard it is for us.

Charlie has experienced so much in his young life already, from zip lining to riding elephants in Thailand, to hiking up waterfalls, to snorkelling in underwater caves. He has the daredevil in him, and I love him for that!
Letting Charlie live his life as he grows into a teen gets considerably more of a challenge.

Even before knowing about Charlie's condition, I knew I'd struggle with this one. I am a self-confessed control freak with a perfectionist thrown in. This is a tough combo to have and usually results in me making life much harder for myself and sometimes those around me!

If you have had a teenager, then I'm sure you will appreciate this. We want our kids to have the most incredible, fulfilling, happiest and healthiest version of life that they can. The mistakes that we may have made ourselves we want them to avoid. This isn't realistic and I do appreciate that I'm not helping either of my boys if I don't let them make their own mistakes.

I remember my dad telling me that he had always thought that I'd travel the world. While he didn't say that he was disappointed I felt that he was. This frustrated me as I felt I had achieved quite a lot in my life at that point (I also had visited many different countries around the world) and I promised myself that I would try my very hardest to not put my own feelings and desires on my boys. I know that my dad just wanted the best for me.

I truly want them to both be healthy and happy……anything else is the icing on the cake!

The problem with having a teenager is that they are desperate to have new experiences, they feel like they are an adult but aren't quite there with always making the best decisions. They have friendships where they can easily be influenced and quite often don't want to stand out or be different.

Only recently I had an experience that is up there in terms of me having to let Charlie take the responsibility for his own decisions.
It was during his GCSEs that he had a day of no exams and there was a large group of his friends all

going off to the park. It was a beautiful boiling hot day, and I knew that the allure of the lake would be a big part of his day. We had already had experience of him jumping into one of the lakes unbeknown to me at the time, so I was very concerned.

I talked about my concerns about open water swimming and the fact that it could be dangerous even without considering his epilepsy.
I showed him articles in which, not just children but also adults, had lost their lives whilst swimming in lakes. It broke my heart when he told me that he realised all of this, but he still wanted to go in. We had quite a few heated words to say the least. I slowly realised though that I would not always be there for Charlie, that he could even go off on holiday next year without me there by his side.

Considering the fact that we had been told by his consultant to not even leave him alone in the bath for fear of drowning you can imagine my anxiety. What could I do? Other than lock him in his room and forbid him to go? Even doing this wouldn't stop him from doing it another time.
I like to think that I have a very honest relationship with both boys. They know that they can always come and ask us anything and our relationship is based on trust.

I explained this to Charlie. I didn't want him to tell me what I wanted to hear to then go ahead and do it anyway.
I explained to him that even if he was swimming with me and his dad, we would still struggle to get him out of the water mid seizure. Not only is taller than I am now but because of the nature of his fits, the jerking and stiffness of his limbs, it's very hard to get him into a safe position anyway.

This particular day I was working further away from home, and I can honestly say it was one of the hardest days of work I had ever experienced. I had to teach a whole school a healthy eating cooking experience, so the times were very tight and I had very little time to think about anything. I felt completely powerless to be able to help Charlie. Let's face it, even if I was home, I would be unable to help Charlie if he had a fit in the lake.

If you are reading this and thinking that I'm a really bad mum for "letting him do this" I totally get it, totally understand why you think this. I believe as parents we have to take a step back and let our children make their own decisions, even if they aren't the right ones. We all learn by our mistakes? Suffice to say Charlie was ok, he did go in the lake, and he kept in touch with us to let us know he was ok.
Funnily enough he hasn't been in the lake since, and I hope that by allowing him to make his own

decision, it has taken off the shine and excitement of a forbidden activity.

There are so many obstacles to get through as your child grows up. There is the allure of alcohol and drugs, the worry of their safety whilst out and not with you. All we can do is to equip them with the right tools, to talk things through so that they have an idea on coping strategies.

Chapter 27

We all know self-care is important, particularly if you're a parent but even more so if you have a child that has a condition like epilepsy. Easier said than done I know. There are times when I've wondered if I've lived off my nerves alone! It's no surprise if you've experienced so many seizures. They come with no warning, can be extremely dramatic; particularly if the person having the fit hurts themselves. Family or friends have asked me what it looks like and if you haven't experienced it, it's like your child is taken over by a poltergeist. They are unrecognisable as their features are distorted with their eyes rolling back and their limbs are rigid in a fixed position. I'm sure everyone's different and how Charlie looks mid fit may be very different to your loved one. Quite often we are alerted to Charlie having a fit by a loud crash. This may be a piece of furniture he's fallen into or him falling to the floor. As you may be able to imagine when you live in a house with two boys and a dog, loud crashes can be a common occurrence. The number of times I've rushed up the stairs thinking Charlie was having a seizure to find that he'd dropped something is unreal. Unfortunately, there have been plenty of occasions that my fears have also been confirmed. We are fortunate in many respects as Charlie tends to have a seizure within an hour or so of waking up. This is not a guarantee as he has had a few seizures at other times during the day but at least it gives us an idea. The downside of this is that I'm on eggshells during the morning. When you're on high alert like this for a long period of time you can feel quite tired and drained. This is why self-care is so important. There are lots of different things you can do:

Tell someone about how you feel. Sometimes we are so caught up in what's happening in our lives we live on auto pilot and don't give ourselves time to check in on our emotions. The number of times I chat to family or friends about what's happening and they quite often come up with a suggestion that's staring me in the face. If we are so close to a situation it's sometimes hard to see the wood for the trees. Talking to others helps bring a fresh perspective. If you don't want to be given a solution, it's still good to talk and unleash how you are feeling. When we keep everything all pent up then that's when it's unhealthy. It can feel very selfish when we "indulge" in self-care but if you need to be the strong protector then you need time to rebuild and strengthen too.

If you're not comfortable with talking to friends or family I totally get it! I often have felt like the moaner, the doom and gloom merchant, or the one filled with drama. If this is the case, there are lots of different organisations out there that want to help. Quite often these organisations are made up of people that have experienced epilepsy themselves, so they truly understand. There are forums where you can chat with other families or carers that totally understand where you are at and how you are feeling.

Write a journal I wish someone had given me this advice.......It would certainly have helped me to write this book!

Whilst I didn't journal, I did track every seizure. I kept it quite simple with the date, time and where we were. Just seeing that small sentence takes me back to every single one. The one where I'd been teaching on-line and after coming off, I peeped through the glass to the other room that Charlie had been in. He was slumped unconscious on the settee. Imagine my horror and rush of guilt that came over me. I'd been laughing and joking with the children in my class whilst Charlie had been going through all that only in the other room.

Another time, Andy and I were sitting downstairs one midweek evening watching some TV. I could hear something vibrating ever so slightly from upstairs. It wasn't a loud noise at all, and I'm amazed we noticed it over the TV. I went up to investigate and to my complete horror I found Charlie fitting in the smallest gap between his bed and the radiator. It still makes me cold all over to think of this one. I was only grateful that he hadn't harmed himself and he was safe.

So, whilst I didn't journal, I did track dates and times. It was by doing this that we began to notice a pattern. We noticed that whenever Charlie had a seizure, it usually happened within an hour to an hour and a half of him waking. Whilst this hasn't been true for every single seizure, it certainly was the case for 90%. This gave us an insight into the possibility that Charlie's trigger may be tiredness. I'd always been a bit of a fanatic when it came to sleep. Partly because I'm terrible without sleep and can't function very well at all. Andy had read a book all about sleep and we learnt how sleep is the absolute foundation for our health and well-being.

If you can document somewhere when the seizures occur, you can use a timeline and begin to notice patterns yourself. Tiredness and stress can be factors for many of those suffering.

Hormones have played a massive part in Charlie's epilepsy. Whilst he was only nine when he was diagnosed, I believe his hormones had started to kick in. Charlie was quite young when he started puberty, and it was no coincidence that his epilepsy came about at the same time.

If you do start to journal, a massive benefit of doing so is for your own mental wellbeing. It helps you offload, to gather your thoughts and emotions. It can be really therapeutic to start journaling. My main reason for starting this book was to help others. My heart goes out to each and every one of you that is going through this journey. Even if your journey is different to mine, it can still be a very lonely place. I don't want you to feel alone, I'm with you a million per cent. I told myself that even if no one read my book then it was still worth doing for my own sanity. To get all of my thoughts and experiences down into one place means so much to me.

Don't compare This is advice we all get when looking at our kids' development and it's likely that it really comes into play when your child has Epilepsy. One of the biggest challenges I've felt with Charlie and his condition is not feeling I am able to encourage him to be as independent as I'd like him to be. I look back at when I was his age and it's scary how much more streetwise I was. Part of this is because I was a girl and I think girls can be more independent and grow up more quickly. It also is down to our family set up. The fact is that when I was 16, I had two younger brothers and a younger sister to help look after. I had to grow up quicker and that's just a fact of life. Unfortunately, when it comes to Epilepsy, I feel like you have to second guess every eventuality and I've struggled to feel comfortable leaving Charlie on his own. We are fortunate in the fact that 99% of his seizures happen within the first hour of his waking but this isn't a given. If there have been occasions that I've had to leave him whilst at work I've tried my absolute best to minimise risk. This would mean asking him to stay in his bed until I'm home (luckily, I'm self-employed and only ever out for an hour or so at a time) not to shower or go downstairs. I can't tell you how my mind has gone into overdrive thinking of all different horrific scenarios from him falling down the stairs, knocking himself out in the shower, or worse. Whilst this is how we've had to adjust the way we live our lives, working around Epilepsy, it can be very hard if I was to compare with other friends that have children of a similar age. It serves no purpose wishing that we were able to switch off and leave our teens at home to fend for themselves, but we are only human and it's natural to do so. I've noticed that as Charlie has crept into his teens this side of life has got harder.

Whilst other kids his age were maybe allowed to have a beer at a family BBQ or catch-up, we've felt very cautious about this. How could we allow our boy to consume alcohol when he was on the amount of meds that he was on? Would him having alcohol disrupt his sleep and cause seizures? Charlie was around 15 when he started to go to parties, and he didn't seem to mind at first that the majority of his friends were allowed to have a drink. This didn't last long though and I'll always remember when he asked me how long he'd have to wait until he could do the same? I would have laughed if it wasn't so tragic....he asked this as we were walking down the path from his friends after a sleep-over. The fact he'd just had a seizure and his friend's mum had called me to let me know yet this was the first thing on his mind was quite telling! That's teenagers for you I guess! Like any parent we don't get a book on how to best parent, we navigate through the choppy waters as best we can. We make decisions based on our judgement as well as a little of how we were brought up ourselves. My mum and dad had always been very liberal with me as I grew up. They let me have a drink or two when I was with them and allowed me to go to clubs and pubs. Their ethos was all based on honesty. If they knew where I was, I would be more likely to call them and ask for help if I needed it! I had many friends who felt that they had to lie to their parents as they were so very strict with them. This wasn't what I wanted for our boys. I always wanted them to feel they could ask us anything about life and never to feel afraid of telling us if they were in trouble.

It was only recently as Charlie turned 16 that I began to think about the possibility of the fact that Charlie may have to learn to live with Epilepsy and that he may not grow out of it. By this point he was having seizures on average every 2-3 weeks. His sleep was closely monitored, and he was never put in the position of late nights, yet he'd still have seizures.

One of these occurrences that sticks in my mind is the morning of his DofE expedition. For those that are not familiar with DofE it's The Duke of Edinburgh award. You spend 3-6 months learning a new skill or activity as well as taking part in volunteer work. Whilst Charlie was undertaking his DofE we were hit by the pandemic, so the expedition part of the award was put back by over 12 months. When we were finally given the green light of a date, we had lots of chats with school with regards to how we could keep Charlie safe. The expedition consisted of two days orienteering and an overnight stay in a tent - boy heaven! His school was going to give his team walkie talkies so they could alert members of staff if there was a problem as well as a tracker in his bag if they needed to locate where he was.

It felt like such a big deal letting Charlie go and I was so very nervous about anything happening. I knew we had to do this for his own sake, and it would do him the absolute world of good. I also felt incredibly guilty about the other boys in his team. It wasn't fair to ask 16-year-old boys to take responsibility for Charlie. The other parents were amazing, so unbelievably supportive but this didn't take away the nagging feeling that they'd have felt relieved if Charlie wasn't there.

The night before the expedition Charlie was all packed up, excited, and raring to go. He didn't even put up a fight when I suggested he went to bed early, even earlier than a school night! It was a Friday night, so I was impressed.

We got up early the following day and I was watching him like a hawk. He'd had over eight hours sleep, which would be enough for most people, but I'd known him to have seizures with a similar amount of sleep the night before. I even put his huge rucksack on my back and carried it down the stairs for him - I couldn't shake images of him having a seizure whilst walking down the stairs with that on his back!

I began to relax when we had around 15 minutes to go before we needed to leave. As Charlie was tucking into his porridge, it began, he began to have a seizure. I couldn't believe it; we were so close to getting him there and it was all so cruelly taken away from him. As he was perched on a bar stool as the seizure began, I rushed around to where he was, and rugby tackled him to the floor. The stool came crashing down with us, but I needed to break his fall. Because of the fact he was eating pre the seizure happening he began to choke as he had a mouth full of porridge. I was desperately trying to scoop everything out of his mouth. This was no mean feat as he was grinding his teeth and it was very hard to get into his mouth, not least because he kept biting me. It's (one) of my top fears when it comes to Charlie's seizures.

Whilst Charlie was fitting prior to his DofE trip, it was the first time that I broke down and cried whilst trying to help him. Tears of frustration and despair over this cruel condition. Why could it not let him live his life? Why did it have to rear its ugly head every time? Why did it have the power to spoil so many things?
It was only 10 minutes until we were due to leave the house, I needed to call school to let them know Charlie wouldn't be making it. I didn't want to call them; I was trying to figure if there was a way we could make it still happen. Was there a way Charlie could perhaps join them later? Of course, there was no way he could. He needed sleep, rest and recovery. He certainly didn't need a 25 mile walk with a sleepless night in a tent.

Later on, I would realise that him having the fit in the safety and comfort of home was the best outcome. If it had happened on the coach or whilst away with school, it would have been so public. It would have caused a lot of worry for the kids and teachers. Above everything Charlie could keep his privacy and that was so important to him and us.

Charlie experienced seizures at different times of the day and they were a combination of absent and partial as well as full tonic clonic. If you're unsure of the difference between the two, I'll explain from my own perspective rather than the official classification:

Partial/absent seizures
These are more subtle than the tonic clonic seizures. The person experiencing the seizure is fully conscious but quite often unable to communicate. They can potentially appear to be ignoring you. Sometimes they sit or stand stock still yet other times they can still be actually standing or walking. I can vividly remember a couple of times that Charlie experienced one of these. One of them was when I walked in the house after going out shopping. I was calling out to find out where Charlie was. He wasn't answering me, yet I knew he was in the house. I had actually walked straight past him in the lounge but because he was sitting so still, and he couldn't tell me he was there I hadn't realised. When I realised what was happening, I was incredibly upset. I gently rolled him onto his side. His eyes were pleading with me to understand but no words were coming out. He told me afterwards that he felt like he was trapped inside his own body. He was around 10 at the time. Whilst these types of seizures are easier for us to witness, I think they are very scary for the person that's experiencing them. If you experience partial seizures, it can be difficult for others around to realise what's happening. Teachers or colleagues

may not realise that you are epileptic and may assume you cannot hear them or are being ignorant.

Full tonic clonic seizures

These used to be referred to as Grand Mal seizures. They are the most dramatic and potentially dangerous, as Charlie will fall to the ground unconscious. His limbs become very stiff and there's a lot of jerky, involuntary movements. Quite often he can drool and whilst his eyes are open, he can't see or remember anything. Sometimes people that experience this kind of seizure will wet themselves but luckily for Charlie this has never happened. I thank my lucky stars every single day that Charlie has never badly injured himself. He has broken his front teeth a few times, cut his head open and plenty of bruises but other than that he has come out relatively unscathed. We have found him in a variety of different positions, including falling backwards off a chair, falling into a bath, sliding into the smallest gap between his bed and the wall, as well as falling off a high bar stool.

The majority of his clonic tonics have been at home, but he has had a few landings on the pavement on the way to school as well as in the car.

Whilst it had become apparent to us that Charlie's trigger was tiredness and you'd be forgiven for thinking that this could be quite easy to avoid but by the time we realised this fact Charlie was a teenager. If you're a teenager, then you're not really into early nights! It wasn't even as if he had the seizures after really late nights; it could sometimes be if he had his full eight hours!

Join a support group There are so many different support groups out there for those that are living with Epilepsy. This goes for those that have the condition themselves or for those that are caring for someone that has it. Given the choice, I'd happily take away Charlie having Epilepsy to have it for myself. I remember him telling me that he wished he could take my endometriosis away and he'd suffer with it rather than see me live with the condition.

It's very hard to watch someone whom you love so much have attacks. In many ways I feel that Louie has gone through so much as he has witnessed 99% of Charlie's seizures from a young age. Only until recently has he been able to stay in the same room whilst it happens as it frightened him so much. It really is a whole family issue and one that we all have grown to live with.

So back to the support groups....

Whilst I did enrol onto an Epilepsy support forum, I didn't get actively involved which I do regret. I offered Charlie the opportunity to get involved as I thought it might help him to connect with others of a similar age that live with the condition. He didn't feel it was something that he wanted to participate with at the time and I respected this.

Part of the reason I didn't take my own advice was because I managed to connect with another parent at Charlie's secondary school. At the time I had a cookery school on a Saturday morning that was based at Charlie's future secondary school. I noticed there was some information regarding a pupil that was already attending the school regarding what to do in the event of him having an episode.
When Charlie was granted a place at the school, I got in touch with the school medical officer. During our first meeting to discuss Charlie's needs I passed on my contact details to see if this parent wanted to get in touch.

I'm so very glad she did as we met up a few times and have had lots to chat about. It's so lovely to have this connection with another parent that totally understands what we are going through. We are unbelievably blessed with family and friends that care so much about Charlie, but there are many times that I fear I am burdening them with my thoughts and fears.

If you have someone in your life that has Epilepsy, then it can take hostage over your mind. It's the hardest thing in the world to switch off from the "what may happen," and the "maybes."

Because of the fact that Charlie's trigger is tiredness then we are on high alert every morning. Every time he gets in the shower I wonder if this is the day that he has a seizure in there. It frightens the hell out of me, and I've asked him a hundred times not to lock the door. He's a teenage boy, he wants his privacy and I totally get it! Even once he's out of the shower I still worry about him having a seizure whilst walking down the stairs. He's had a couple of seizures at the top of the stairs, and I can't help feeling that it's a warning.

One of the worst aspects of Epilepsy in my mind is how it comes up to bite you on the bum when you're least expecting it and we recently had an experience of this.

We'd gone on a family trip to New York as a surprise for Andy's 50th and I was pretty nervous about the risk of Charlie having a seizure either on the plane or whilst we were out there. We had the combination of early starts, jet lag and the tiredness from travelling long haul. The airline had kindly positioned us in extra legroom seats so that if anything happened, we had space to look after Charlie.

We were amazed that he was absolutely fine. We couldn't believe it but were super relieved that there were no dramas, and we could enjoy our trip without Epilepsy rearing its ugly head.

We came home on Thursday morning, so we had a good few days to recover and catch up on sleep. It was the Monday morning when Charlie got up for school that he had a seizure. It was such a shock as he'd not had one for seven months! The longest respite for such a long time. Every time he has a seizure we are completely in shock; you never get used to it. It's so aggressive, it's like a tsunami taking over your life without any warning whatsoever. We can be having a normal conversation and WHAM it happens. This time Charlie was at the top of the stairs after coming out of the shower when he collapsed. Sadly, he cut his head open this time so there was blood everywhere. Nothing ever prepares you for finding your beloved boy in this state - no matter how many times it happens. After a trip to A&E to get checked out he came home to tell the tale.

I can't tell you how proud I am of this boy for how he deals with his condition. He has never actually ever moaned about living with Epilepsy. He has had to put up with so much, so much intervention, so much having to be "different" and more than anything having an OTT mum like me!

Whilst his friends have a carefree life (as they so should) every step of his life we have had to consider. How his meds affect his mindset, what activities he can do without supervision, being out and about on his own or with just his friends. I hope that we have considered all of his life so far without too much fuss. I am fiercely determined that he lives the fullest and best life he can. We have to make adjustments, but I hope they are discreet and with only the bare minimum of people that need to be involved. I do wonder if his resilience was built up from the very start. Being in special care he had so much intervention, from hourly blood tests, machines beeping and the 24-hour circus of noise and people that hospitals have to be. All before he should have even been born. Whilst most babies are in the safety and warmth of their mummies' tummies Charlie was in special care for three months. Maybe he built up his resilience here, maybe he was born that way……who knows?
All I do know is that he was born a fighter, and it is down to him that he has grown into this young man I see before me.

Chapter 28

I value resilience so much……it's up there with loyalty and kindness. I try to explain to my boys that you're not born with resilience, but you build it up as you experience more and more in life. It's one of the things that people around me comment on, how strong I am. I can't say there's much choice about what comes into your life, but I guess we all have a choice on how we react to these occurrences? The nature/nurture debate is something that I am fascinated by. I first learnt about it whilst at Uni alongside Maslow's hierarchy of needs. Little did I realise just a few years later I would be seeing this come to life, in my own life! One of the first times I heard someone remark upon it was when Charlie was having his pre-school booster at the age of three. The nurse couldn't believe how nonplussed Charlie was. He didn't even seem to have noticed he'd had the injection. This nurse was used to children crying and screaming after the injection and Charlie hadn't even flinched! Just 12 months later, Charlie and I were involved in a car crash and as I got Charlie out of his car seat the paramedics couldn't believe how calm he was. I did wonder if he was like this because he was naturally a resilient child or if it was because of the intervention he'd experienced within the first three months of his life. From the very beginning, he was subjected to multiple blood tests every day. Because of how early he was born they had to check his vitals 24/7. It was incredibly hard to watch my babies, that should still have been in the warmth and safety inside of me, being subjected to these invasive tests.

Another vivid memory was when the Doctors needed to check the boys' eyesight. They had to use a contraption that forced their paper-thin eyelids open, to run the test. Whilst I understood completely that this was a necessity it just looked so barbaric, something that would look quite at home on a scene of Game of Thrones and not within a special care baby unit.

Looking back Charlie went through so much even before his Epilepsy diagnosis. From having ear grommets fitted, to having a procedure to have a testicle pulled down. There were also worries and concerns over the size of his head that involved him having various tests and procedures. I've lost count of how many hospital visits and ambulance rides he's had. I can't thank all of the medics involved enough. They have the perfect balance of professionalism and light-hearted banter that helps us feel at ease in sometimes very worrying circumstances. These people clearly are carers and want to help others. I've never failed to feel touched by the kindness and thoughtfulness for us as parents. I still remember specific individuals that have looked after us from years ago. An example of this human kindness was when one of the special care nurses sent us two personalised baubles for Christmas. Even though Charlie and Tom were born in April and we left SCBU at the end of July, this beautiful soul sent us two baubles to hang on our tree five months later. A tribute to Tom that means he will never leave our side.

So back to Charlie's resilience.....I guess we'll never really know why he is so resilient. It's likely a combination of his genetics as well as his experiences. He's had to put up with so much in his 16 years so far. Not just medically, but also socially. From junior school feeling different, having his mum follow him around on school trips, his friends having to escort him to the toilet. He's taken it all in his stride. I guess he's not known any different.

Chapter 29

A special mention has to go to Louie. Louie has seen so much in his young life with Charlie's Epilepsy. I would go so far as to say that he has witnessed 90% of Charlie's seizures. I have always tried to remain calm for Louie's sake. If he sees that we are calm, he is less likely to get anxious himself. In the beginning he would cry out and rush out of the room. Even now at 15 and seeing Charlie mid seizure countless times, he will always prefer to look the other way. He is very insightful and quite often will spot that Charlie is about to go into a fit. I've tried to show him what he needs to do so that if we are ever out and he's home alone with Charlie he will feel confident in looking after Charlie. The day so far has still not occurred, but I am sure it will at some point.

I remember one day during half term that Louie had popped out whilst Charlie was home alone but had forgotten to take his key. He rang the doorbell countless times whilst calling for his brother through the letterbox. When he rang me to tell me, I wasn't near home so I asked one of my friends if they could pop by to check everything was ok as they had a key. I was on tenterhooks waiting to hear if he was ok, my mind going into overdrive over what my friend would be greeted with. Needless to say, Charlie was completely fine and was wearing his air pods so couldn't hear when the doorbell rang……. talk about an unnecessary drama! I have always worried about Louie being traumatised over what he has experienced during these past years, but I am hoping that he will benefit later in life. He is far less likely to worry when there is an emergency and hopefully will be the cool, calm and collected person should anything happen. He has such a level head on his shoulders, and I am so unbelievably proud of the young man he is.

Chapter 30

It's so very important to me that I help others wherever I can. As we've experienced so much as a family, I really do believe that by sharing my own experiences I can help people feel less alone. I think one of the hardest aspects of going through trauma can be the feeling of loneliness or that no-one else has gone through what you are going through. As I said right at the beginning of this book, if I can help even just one person by writing this book then I'm happy.

Below are some of my biggest learnings:

Gratitude
Now before you start rolling your eyes, please hear me out on this one. I'm relatively new to the world of journaling and gratitude but I wish I'd started earlier. I honestly believe that if you search hard enough you will find the positive in most occurrences. If you can get into the habit of daily gratitude, it gets easier and easier. I have a book that I write in every morning and every evening. It asks me different questions each day, so it never gets boring. Even if I have a really full-on day, it helps me think about what I can be grateful for. This may be something as small as feeling grateful for my coffee or looking forward to sitting down later to watch our favourite box set. I will also practise gratitude in my evening as this helps me

think about what went well in my day or what I could work more on. A great example of gratitude was when Charlie had his seizure just five minutes before going on his DofE trip. I was initially completely gutted for him and all of the work that had taken place to keep him safe for his trip beforehand. After the initial shock and disappointment, I realised that it had happened at the best time. Far better that it had happened at home where he could keep his privacy and I was there to cushion his fall. He would have hated it if it had happened on the coach in front of everyone. Equally, it would have been catastrophic if he had had a seizure in the middle of nowhere. Emergency services would have been called and it would have been traumatic for everyone involved. Practising gratitude on a daily basis really does help when the chips are down, and everything may feel so dark and miserable. As I write this part of our story life is pretty tough with Andy going through so much with his treatment for Cancer, both boys going through their exams and so much of things that we enjoy have been taken away from us. Am I really miserable? Do I hate my life? In my head and heart, I actually feel pretty upbeat and positive each day. The reason for this is that I know I cannot control the Cancer or how teenage hormones can sometimes get a little too much. What I can control is my own self-care and look after my own mindset. If I am in a good place, then I am in a much better position to be the best Mum and Wife I can be!

Don't be afraid to be yourself

Now this may sound like a real obvious one but chatting to others I do get the impression that some people are afraid of being themselves, afraid of being different. Looking back, I guess a big part of the reason I resisted going alcohol free was because 99% of my circle of friends drank. I didn't want to be different; I didn't want to stick out or be the awkward person that wasn't going into the kitty or drinking the same drink. It's interesting now that I don't drink, that I have discovered lots of other people don't either. There are some people that will go out and drink a cup of tea, some that will drive and some that will have just one glass of wine. Not everyone is drinking, and it really shouldn't define us. I don't want to be "the woman that doesn't drink." I'd like to think that I have far more about me than that. I wish I could have told my younger self to not worry about what others think. I honestly feel that the older I get, the less bothered I am! I know that my family and friends who know me best will stick by me through thick and thin and I don't need to have to explain myself. I am extremely fortunate as I have a brilliant support network through my close family members as well as friendships that have spanned over almost 30 years. I also have other newer friendships that I have made later on in my life that are incredibly important to me. They are not defined by the length of time that we have known each other. These friendships skip the duration of years as they are made after becoming a parent and when we are more sure of the person we have become. They are brutally honest friendships. For anyone that knows me, they will know that honesty is at the core of all I am.

Compartmentalise

So, I think I learnt to do this first when I was so poorly after having Louie. I knew it would take all of my strength to get myself back to fighting fit and be released to come home. I also knew how heartbreaking it was to think about not being with my boys. The guilt I initially had over not being with Charlie for so long was dreadful. To further deepen this guilt, I couldn't believe how little I was able to be with Louie when he was in special care. I knew how important it was to have skin to skin care with Louie and what a massive difference it could make to him if I was able to breastfeed. I was unable to do either for him; the guilt felt like it would kill me. Very early on I realised that this guilt was making me ill and not helping me in my recovery after the surgery. I had to put the boys to the furthest part of my mind, knowing that they were being very well looked after and all I needed to do was look after myself so that I could be released from hospital. I think this way of focusing on just one aspect of your life at a time could be really helpful for many of us. It can be applied to all areas of our life, whether it's work, family or even our own personal development. For me, it's about setting my intentions and sticking to it. It doesn't come naturally though, particularly if you are trying to squash maternal feelings. I guess for me, it was about putting my desire to be with my boys right to the back of my mind as I knew worrying would hinder my recovery and ultimately make my time away from them further.

Listen to your gut

This is most possibly the biggest lesson that I learnt. How often have you heard the phrase "listen to your gut"?! There is a reason for this as your gut will let you know if something is a good idea or not. The day that Tom died, I ignored my gut. My gut told me that all was not well when I called the hospital up on that fateful day. Not for one minute am I saying that I could have stopped Tom from dying, but something somewhere was trying to tell me that all was not well. When I realised that my gut had been trying to tell me to get back up to hospital, even though the nurse told me everything was ok, I pushed the nagging feeling to one side. I promised myself after this that I would never again ignore my gut. It can often be really silly things like, have I closed the front door properly or switched the oven off? It can also be for the big decisions I'm making in life. If I am at a crossroads or needing to make a decision, I will ask my gut for some assistance. It hasn't let me down since.

Don't compare

Now this is a tough one and one that's definitely a work in progress for me. We all do it, whether it's based on what test results our kids have got at school or how lovely other people's houses are. I get very envious of how clean other people's houses are! Don't get me wrong, I'd like to think our house is (fairly) clean but It's very much lived in home. We have two teenage boys and a messy dog in the mix, so I just don't get stressed about it anymore. I find it hard to work in a messy room so if I'm short on time I will tidy the room I'm in and worry about the rest of the house another time! This means that my kitchen that I spend most of the time in is usually pretty tidy and the rest of upstairs is less so. Going back to not comparing with others; it is so very important. We don't know what is going on behind closed doors. The images that our friends and family share on social media are the ones that they want us to see. They don't show us two minutes after the family shot has been taken when a big tantrum occurs. It's for this reason that so many people come off social media because they don't feel good about themselves as it feels like everyone around them is having the best of times. I'm super conscious of the fact that I use social media to share what Pudding and Pie is up to as visibility is so very important. Not for one minute does it mean that I have the perfect life. We tend to envy the one thing in other people's lives that we feel we lack in ourselves. This is crazy thinking as we can't all be brilliant at everything and whilst you may be comparing how organised your one friend is, it's highly likely that she wishes she was more laid back like you! I guess for me it's about celebrating the person we are and that's the whole person, warts and all!

One step at a time

This one is particularly challenging for anyone in business. Naturally we are most likely to be full of different ideas all at once and can be impatient. I am a massive perfectionist and hate when there are blockages in my way, or I've not completed the tasks that I have set for myself. I've realised at the grand old age of 46 that our feelings are just a snapshot of time. If I have a bad day, then that's all that it is. The next day will be different, and I try not to overthink it. Sometimes we have such high expectations of ourselves and how each and every day should feel and that is just unrealistic. We will have boring, tedious, funny, easy, quiet, busy, and stressful days but they are just that: a moment in time. It's like the analogy where, if every day was spent on holiday, then it wouldn't be a holiday. If every day was magical, would it stay magical? We need to have the contrast of days being different or not so good for us, to really appreciate the good days, right? Living in the moment is such a big part of this for me. Enjoy each moment that you are doing work that you enjoy, spending time with people you love and not to worry or think about what anyone else is doing.

The last word

So, if you've got to this bit of the book, I applaud you! It means so very much to me that you've taken the time to read my little story. I hope that you have taken some of the lessons that I have learnt and maybe they can help you in this thing called life? I am so very grateful for the experiences I have had so far, and I feel that I have achieved a great deal, but equally I believe there is far more to come. It feels like I'm only just starting out; I want to achieve and make a bigger impact upon so many others' lives. If I was run over by a bus tomorrow, I would honestly feel happy about what I have achieved during my life so far....... not that I want to die for a very, very long time yet! I have far more I want to experience and achieve.

Watch this space!

• • •

If you have enjoyed reading my little book, please write me a review even if it's just one word as it means the world to me.